AUSTIN HEALEY 100

THE ORIGINAL 4-CYLINDER MODELS

John Wheatley

CONTENTS

ISBN 0 85429 487 2

A FOULIS Motoring Book

First published 1986

© **Haynes Publishing Group**

Published by:
Haynes Publishing Group,
Sparkford, Near Yeovil,
Somerset BA22 7JJ

Haynes Publications Inc.
861 Lawrence Drive, Newbury
Park, California 91320, USA

British Library Cataloguing in Publication Data

Wheatley, John
  Austin-Healey 100 (original 4-cylinder model)
  –(Super profile)
  1. Austin-Healey automobile–History
  I. Title   II. Series
  629.2'222   TL215.A92
  ISBN 0-85429-487-2

Library of Congress Catalog Card Number

85-82155

Editor: Rod Grainger
Cover design: Rowland Smith
Page layout: Peter Kay
Series photographer:
Andrew Morland
Road tests: Courtesy of *Autosport
Motor, Road & Track*
Printed in England by:
J.H. Haynes & Co. Ltd

Further titles in this series will be published at regular intervals. For information on new titles please contact your bookseller or write to the publisher.

FOREWORD

I was a sixth form schoolboy when I saw my first Healey car in a Birmingham showroom in 1947, and I remember the sense of awe I felt when looking at this new postwar car. Guaranteed to exceed 100mph, it represented a tremendous design advance over the majority of cars just beginning to come back onto the UK market (in the main carried over pre-war models of mediocre performance) and it quickly established the name of Healey as the builders of high quality, high performance vehicles. When the Silverstone appeared it was obviously a car for the serious competition driver and was much admired for its purposeful appearance.

The "100" was a startling new concept from Healey. Less expensive than previous Warwick products and planned to be built in rather larger volumes, it represented a great leap forward in specification, design and performance in relation to the MG TC I was driving at the time of the new Healey's announcement. Sleek and incredibly beautiful, the "100" was a proper sports car, capable of being driven in the street and being used in serious competition; as endorsed by its subsequent Le Mans début a few months later.

Donald Healey and his family, who together typify those classic English entrepreneurs who seem to succeed at everything they attempt, were able to create the Austin-Healey marque which has since given great pleasure to enthusiasts the world over. It is fortunate that their cars were designed and manufactured in the two decades after the end of World War Two when manufacturers were able to bring their ideas to fruition without the restrictions of today. Current legislation attaching to automobile design means that we shall never again see the like of the Austin-Healey and its contemporaries. Modern cars are very efficient, safe, and fast, but lack the charisma of the muscular "Big Healey". Fortunately, we have preserved many of the cars which have earned the name Healey an honoured place in International motoring history.

It has given me great pleasure to write this book and the reader will fairly quickly realise that I hold the Austin-Healey 100 in great affection. It is a car which has given my family and me much enjoyment over more than thirty years and has opened the doors to many good and valued friendships. In writing this book I have been fortunate to have the help of many people, but special thanks must go to Anders Clausager of The British Motor Industry Heritage Trust, who made available to me the recently recovered microfilm of Longbridge production Job Cards, allowing new and original research to be carried out and published here for the first time. I have to thank

Austin Rover for the use of photographic archive material; David Matthews for providing an up to date listing of overseas clubs; *Autocar, Road & Track, Autosport* and *Motor* magazines for permission to reproduce original contemporary road test material; John Reed and Gerry Hills for allowing Andrew Morland to photograph their cars, and Ian Walker for providing period photographs of his car. I am indebted to Paul Skilleter, Marek Szpalski, Roger Moment and Stuart Johnson for the use of photographs from their own personal collections. I am very grateful to Peter Tanser and Roger Moment for their contributions to the "Owner's View" Section which should encourage all potential owners. Their enthusiasm confirms the belief that the Austin-Healey 100 remains an attractive and enjoyable sports car, evocative of an era never to return.

Above all, I must thank my wife Heather for her help and encouragement. She is as interested in our Healey as I am, which makes me a lucky man indeed!

John Wheatley

HISTORY

At its announcement, the Healey 100 was the sensation of the 1952 London Motor Show, but it is doubtful if anyone at that time anticipated the enduring admiration and affection it would command through the following three decades up to the present day. An enthusiasm which shows every indication of being sustained by future generations of enthusiasts around the world.

The idea of the Healey 100 was conceived by Donald Healey following a visit to the United States in 1951. He envisaged a model to fill the gap in the sports car market between the MG "T" types and the more expensive but much faster Jaguar XK models. The principal product objectives were that it should have obvious sporting characteristics; be strong, reliable and constructed from proven readily available major mechanical units; be easy to maintain; have stylish appearance; be capable of 100mph and be priced at under 3000 US Dollars exclusive of taxes. These objectives were successfully achieved in the creation of the Healey 100.

The Donald Healey Motor Company was established at "The Cape" in the town of Warwick and in October 1946, began the production of its first two models,

the Westland-bodied Tourer and Elliott-bodied Saloon, which shared the same chassis and mechanical units. Facilities were limited and volumes were low, with a combined total of 165 cars being built until the models were superseded in October 1950 by the 2-door 4-seat Tickford-bodied Saloon and the Abbott-bodied drophead coupé derivative. These two models continued in production until early 1954, with a total of 301 units built.

In parallel with the continuing production of the two original Healey cars, a number of other derivatives were developed on the standard chassis, and sold over the same period. After two years production of the Westland and Elliott models, the more spacious Sportsmobile convertible was announced in October 1948. Offering a very high level of passenger comfort with 100mph performance but somewhat lacking in style, this car was the least successful Healey and was discontinued early in 1950 after only 23 examples had been built. In the Spring of 1949 the development of the first true Healey sports car, the Silverstone, was begun. Announced in July of the same year, the Silverstone was based on the usual Healey chassis, Riley power unit and rear axle, with a lightweight stressed-skin bodyshell providing minimal creature comforts. It was 150lb lighter than previous Cape products and had a top speed of around 110mph, a third gear maximum of 80mph and a zero to 60mph time of 11 seconds. Its high performance and safe handling characteristics made it a very successful competition car on both sides of the Atlantic, resulting in its becoming the best known of all the Warwick-built cars despite its short production run of only 105 units before September 1950 when it was discontinued to make way for the Nash-Healey.

The Nash-Healey derives from a chance meeting between Donald

Healey and George Mason, President of the Nash Kelvinator Corporation of America, when both were aboard the liner *Queen Elizabeth en route* to the United States in December 1949.

The success of the Silverstone in America showed the requirement in that market for a larger-engined model and so an agreement was made between the two men for Nash engines, transmissions and rear axles to be supplied to Warwick for fitting to a slightly modified Healey chassis with a British-built body. The prototype car was completed in April 1950 and entered in the classic Mille Miglia road race. This test was successfully completed and was followed by entry into the Le Mans 24 hour race. Despite being involved in an accident and sustaining some damage to the suspension, the car finished fourth overall and was the first British car to finish. Having proven the combination of American mechanical units and Healey chassis in harsh competition, the decision to begin series production was taken in the summer of 1950. The new car was announced at the London Motor Show in October 1950 and made its American début at the February 1951 Chicago Show. Sold exclusively in America the Nash-Healey became the Warwick factory's largest production volume model with 506 units built between December 1950 and August 1954. Initially the cars were fitted with British-designed bodies manufactured by Panelcraft of Birmingham, but from February 1952 the rolling chassis assembly was sent to Pininfarina in Turin to be bodied and then shipped directly to the United States. At the same time, an improved engine was also fitted, lifting the power available from 125 to 135bhp. For 1953 a fixed head coupé version was introduced alongside the convertible model.

Because the Nash-Healey was for export only it was decided to meet anticipated U.K. demand for a similar sized car by introducing the Sports Convertible model at the London Motor Show in October 1951. Essentially a replica Nash-Healey with revised radiator grille and bumpers, the Nash engine was replaced by a six cylinder 3.0 litre Alvis unit developing 106bhp. With bodywork again by Panelcraft, this car was a very high quality product with wind-up windows and easily erected hood. Although in production until late 1953 only 25 were built.

With a full order book for the Nash-Healey, the cash flow through the business was now adequate to permit Donald Healey and his team to capitalize on their accumulated experience and set about the development of what they saw as a new concept in sports car design. Up to this time, all Healey cars had been quite expensive and consequently beyond the reach of many enthusiasts. The new car was planned as a less expensive, straightforward high performance vehicle capable of being built in larger numbers than hitherto. The gestation period began in late 1951 and culminated in the announcement of the Healey 100 in October 1952.

Given the agreed product objectives, one of the first problems to be resolved had to be a choice of power unit since it was known that the Riley engine was going out of production in the fairly near future. Eventually the 2.6-litre Austin A90 engine was picked. This unit was readily available and of proven reliability, following the seven days and nights endurance record breaking run at Indianapolis with the Atlantic Coupé in April 1949. Consequent upon the choice of the Austin engine was the decision to also use the Austin A70/90 derived drive train and running gear components since these were not only cheaper than the traditional Healey-designed parts,

especially the front suspension, but were freely available too.

Having fixed the mechanical specification the next step was to design a suitable chassis. Following Healey design philosophy this was a simple yet strong ladder-type frame with square section parallel side members set 17 inches apart by parallel front and rear box section cross members and braced by a robust box section cruciform centre member and welded-in floor plates. Front and rear scuttle structures were also welded to the basic frame to enhance rigidity and torsional stiffness, the front unit being triangulated by struts running forward to the point where the substantial front suspension towers are carried on the side members. The whole structure was very strong without being overweight and provided the rigid frame which Donald Healey regarded as an essential element in achieving good and safe handling qualities in a high performance car.

The most striking feature of the new car was the body design which marked a radical departure from traditional British car styling. It was incredibly handsome with smooth aerodynamic lines uncluttered by external fittings and, in contrast with the slab-sided TRs and XK Jaguars of the day, it was the first UK design to feature the curving "tumblehome" body sides which are now a regular characteristic of current car designs. It had a roomy cockpit, comfortable individual bucket seats and a large lockable luggage compartment. Conceived by Donald Healey and translated into feasible actuality by stylist Gerry Coker, the design was outstanding and well ahead of its time. After over thirty years it still looks marvellous and is only slightly dated by its marginally narrower aspect than is the current fashion. A sensational design which, in the author's opinion, has never been bettered by a volume production car.

Construction of the prototype car proceeded through the summer of 1952 and after brief driving tests of the running chassis it was sent to Tickford at Newport Pagnell to be bodied. Subsequent road testing of the completed car showed that the car was undergeared on the A70 type 4.125 rear axle ratio. As no alternative crownwheel and pinion set was freely available it was decided to fit the then relatively unknown and untried Laycock de Normanville overdrive unit to the back of the gearbox. When brought into operation this device has the effect of providing a step-up ratio to the output shaft which compensates for the low (numerically high!) final drive gearing. After shake-down tests and adjustments had been completed it was time to assess the performance of the car and so in the Autumn of 1952 the Healey team headed for Belgium and the Ostende-Jabbeke highway, the scene of many famous record breaking runs. Fully aware of the publicity value of successful high speed test drives and confident in the product, Donald Healey approached the respected *Autosport* magazine to take part in the planned tests. This was agreed, and the late John Bolster's report fully justifying the model designation "100" appeared in the 24th October issue of the magazine published on the opening day of the 1952 London Motor Show.

After returning from the successful Belgian tests, the car was converted from disc to wire wheels and quickly prepared for presentation at the London Show, taking its place at the last minute on the Healey stand close to the Warwick Road entrance to Earls Court. Although not prominently displayed, the car attracted great attention, becoming the undisputed star of the show despite the presence of many other very expensive and exotic creations.

The enormous interest aroused by the Healey 100 produced several important but unforeseen consequences. Orders placed for the car were so great that to satisfy demand was quite beyond the capability of the Warwick factory, and the level of interest came to the attention of Leonard Lord, Chief Executive of the Austin Motor Company, supplier of the major mechanical assemblies. Realising the capacity limitations of the Healey company and the sales potential of the car as an addition to his product range, Lord approached Donald Healey with the proposal that Austin take over the manufacture of the Healey and back it up with their worldwide sales and service organisation. An agreement was reached between the two men and the car re-named the "Austin-Healey 100" overnight. A new marque was born! The significant result of this agreement was that many more enthusiasts were able to buy an Austin-Healey than would have been the case had production been limited to Cape capacity. The pleasure of owning and driving a thoroughbred sports car was opened up to a much larger market. The shrewd far-sighted business acumen of Leonard Lord in backing bold new design concepts was to be seen again some years later, when he gave his approval to the legendary Mini, the creation of Sir Alex Issigonis, who was also an enthusiastic Austin-Healey owner.

At a U.K. launch price of £850 exclusive of taxes, the Austin-Healey was still not a very cheap car but substantially undercut the Jaguar XK120 (£1130), the Alvis-Healey Convertible (£1400) and the Tickford and Abbott Healeys (around £1200). The M.G. TD was £530, so that the original price objective was neatly achieved. It is interesting to note that the basic price of the 2.4-litre Healey saloon in January 1947 was £1250 whilst the running chassis was available at £900, very expensive prices in those immediate postwar years when a gross annual salary of £1000 per year was regarded as exceptionally good.

In order to meet the urgent requirement for vehicles for both promotional and development work following the launch of the newly named car, the manufacture of twenty pre-production cars was put in hand at the Warwick factory whilst the volume production facility was being prepared at Longbridge. As part of this programme two cars were prepared and entered for the Mille Miglia in the Spring of 1953 as a preliminary to an entry at Le Mans two months later. The initial outing revealed problems with the throttle linkage and clutch plates, which were rectified in time for the classic French 24 hour race for which three cars were prepared with special engine modifications, later to be offered as a tuning kit. In the event, two cars ran, driven by Lockett/Gatsonides and Wilkins/Bequart, finishing 12th and 14th with the Lockett/Gatsonides car averaging 89.7mph for the 2153 miles covered, a very creditable result for both cars.

Whilst this intense activity was going on at Warwick, production was getting under way at Longbridge with the first cars being completed in mid June. As production began to build up towards the budget programme of 100 cars per week it became apparent that the purchasing power of the Austin buying department could affect some economies in manufacturing costs and in July 1953 a reduction of £100 on the basic price of the car was announced, making it very competitive against the MG and TR models. The price of the car remained at this figure until March 1956 when all BMC car prices were subject to a 7.5% increase lifting the cost to £806, exclusive of British Purchase Tax. The extra price increment for the 100M (incorporating Le Mans modifications) was £105 which was also the charge for converting existing customers' cars at The Cape. The U.S. price of the car was 2985 dollars on the East Coast with the 100M at 3275 dollars.

Production of the "100" continued at Longbridge until the summer holiday factory shut down at the end of July 1956 in anticipation of the change over to building the six-cylinder BN4 cars, which were introduced as a result of engine rationalisation programmes deleting the 4-cylinder unit and the improved market potential of a 2-plus-2 body style. Later, all Austin-Healey manufacture was transferred to the sports car factory at Abingdon as part of a further model programme rationalisation.

During its three years production run, the Austin-Healey "100" was a source of great pride for the work people at Longbridge and was a very successful foreign currency earner for the company. By far the largest market was the North American continent with Australia as the next largest, although a long, long way behind in numbers. The UK market supply was somewhat restricted by the need to export as much production as possible and also to some extent by the car's price. At £1100 tax paid it was not a car for *hoi polloi* in the 1950s! The most popular colour was red followed roughly equally by Healey Blue and white and then green and black.

A total of 14,612 cars were built.

EVOLUTION

There were three main phases in the production run of the Austin-Healey 100, these being the Warwick-built pre-production cars, the Longbridge-built BN1 series and the following BN2 series spanning a total of three and a half years from February 1953 to July 1956.

The Warwick-built cars carry chassis serial numbers outside the range of those allocated to cars built at Longbridge, but the body numbers run in sequence from number 1 on the first car up to 14634 on the last one. The first Warwick-built cars were completed in February 1953 with the remainder being completed by the early Summer. Longbridge manufacture began in May 1953 with the first ten cars being completed by 20th June and the prefix BN1 was added to the chassis numbers, beginning at BN1 L 138031.

The "BN" Type Code is derived from the BMC standards for defining passenger car identifications. In this case the letter "B" indicates an engine displacement in the range 2000 to 2999cc whilst the "N" characterises the body type as "2 Seat Tourer". The digits 1 or 2 refer to the model series. Left Hand Drive derivatives carry the letter

"L" after the BN1 or BN2 code, thus BN1L 138031.

At its introduction, the Austin-Healey 100 was a very comprehensively specified motor car and indeed was advertised as "The Sports Car on which all the usual optional extras are standard equipment". Features included overdrive, heater, tonneau cover and wire wheels, all of which were items which had to be ordered as extra to the basic specification on most of its contemporary competitors.

In common with all cars built in substantial numbers, detail changes were made to the specification of the Austin-Healey 100 during its Longbridge production run, reflecting either the need to overcome identified product problems, to ease manufacture or to comply with legal requirements covering construction and use.

The Warwick cars were very much handbuilt and differ in many small details from the volume production cars due to the urgent need to get the first ones completed without waiting for all components to come on full stream from outside suppliers. In particular, they were built with all body panels and doors in aluminium unlike the volume-built cars which have steel wings and door skins.

During the three and a quarter years that the Austin-Healey 100 was manufactured at Longbridge, significant changes were introduced at the following points.

November 1953: $1/2$ inch positive camber rear springs introduced in place of $1/4$ inch negative camber springs at Chassis 148921 LHS and 148987 RHS in order to improve ground clearance.

December 1953: Revised handbrake lever assembly to improve operating clearance between propeller shaft tunnel and lever introduced at Chassis 149903 LHS and 149950 RHS.

Rigid Perspex side screens deleted at Body 1100 with Chassis 149952 in favour of a revised design with hand-signalling flap.

Telescopically adjustable steering column discontinued in favour of a non-adjustable design at Chassis 149930 LHS and 149950 RHS. Consequent upon, and coincident with, this change a slide adjustable driver's seat was introduced instead of the previous fixed type, in order to retain driving position adjustment. To preserve a neat appearance, the slot in the facia panel surrounding the steering column was reduced in width from $2^1/4$ inches to $1^3/4$ inches.

The facia panel was simplified to a single piece pressing at Chassis 151795.

January 1954: Stiffer rear springs introduced from Chassis 152233 LHS and 152420 RHS. These springs were previously offered to special order as part of the Special Tuning Equipment available for competition work. Because the new springs which also embodied a safety eye on the top leaf were thicker than the previous ones, a simultaneous change was introduced to the rear floor panel and the top of the spring shackle boxes to provide adequate clearance between the spring and body under full bump conditions.

February 1954: Revised bonnet lid catch introduced at body 1950 with Chassis 152100.

March 1954: Revised door lock striker introduced at Chassis 152600.

Harder front dampers introduced as standard at Chassis 153855 LHS and 153857 RHS. This damper specification was previously offered as part of the Special Tuning Equipment available for competition work.

May 1954: To avoid the possibility of the terminals on the centrifugal overdrive switch being short-circuited by accidental contact with the inside of the transmission tunnel cover under excessive torque load movement of the power unit, a raised dome is pressed into the tunnel cover in the area above the switch. Change effective from body 3245 with Chassis 155512.

Steel bonnet lid introduced instead of the original aluminium part at body 3397 with Chassis 156120. Part number was unchanged.

June 1954: Steel boot lid introduced instead of the original aluminium part at body 4129 with Chassis 158100. Part number unchanged.

July 1954: Lead hammer introduced as an alternative to a copper hammer in the tool kit from Chassis 159257.

Improved tonneau cover introduced at Body 4606 with Chassis 159339.

August 1954: Improved, stronger roadwheels introduced at Chassis 159802.

Rear reflectors introduced to meet forthcoming legal requirements effective 1st October.

Rear boot lid badge changed from "Austin of England" to "Austin-Healey".

September 1954: Improved door hinges introduced at Body 5001 with Chassis 219046.

October 1954: Improved cockpit heat shielding introduced at Body 5746 with Chassis 219622. To further improve cockpit ventilation the cold air intake trunking was extended forward to a point immediately behind the front radiator grille.

November 1954: Front brake wheel cylinders reduced in diameter from 1 inch to $7/8$ inch in order to improve brake balance. Introduction at Chassis 221404.

Spiral bevel 4.125 ratio (8/33)

rear axle replaced by "C" type hypoid bevel 4.10 ratio (10/41) rear axle. Associated changes were to rear brakes which were increased in width from $13/4$ inches to $21/4$ inches, rear spring "U" bolts, bump stop rubbers and propeller shaft. Change effective from Chassis 221536 with Body 6478.

January 1955: Revised side screens with improved signalling flap introduced at Body 7258 with Chassis 222600.

August 1955: BN1 production ends at BN1 228025 (a home market car finished in blue with blue trim).

BN2 production begins at BN2L 228047, again a blue car, but for the US market in this case. Some pre-production BN2 cars were built with serial numbers in the range 227XXX and 22800X.

Major specification improvements were made to the BN2 series cars when compared with BN1 models. In particular, the much more robust "C" series 4-speed gearbox with overdrive on the top two ratios was introduced, together with wider front brakes, increased from $13/4$ inches to $21/4$ inches, revised rate front springs, taper roller bearings for the front hubs and self parking windscreen wipers. The cut line for the wheel opening in the front wing was raised by $13/4$ inches to allow for increased wheel travel on full bump.

September 1955: Factory "100M" production begins in the Chassis number range 2282XX, for the US market. These cars embody the Le Mans tuning kit options built into a BN2 car. Initial production was in single body colour and not the duo tone scheme introduced when the model was launched on the UK market in October 1955.

October 1955: 100M derivative announced for the UK market and exhibited at the London Motor Show, although the car had been available in the United States ahead of this announcement.

The previously available "Le Mans" Tuning Kit remained as an aftermarket option for existing cars.

November 1955: Improved door to scuttle seal introduced at Body 11143 with Chassis 229180. This modification effectively overcame a persistent water ingress problem.

July 1956: Production ends at Chassis Number BN2L 233455, a white car with black trim, built for the Persian Gulf market without heater. This car carried Body Number 14587. The last UK-specification car was finished in red with red trim and went to the Donald Healey Motor Company. The last "100M" specification car was built in the series 2334XX, finished black with red trim, and went to Casablanca.

The last US specification car was also in the 2334XX series and was finished in red over black with black trim and black hood.

* * *

During production at Longbridge, all Austin-Healey 100 cars were built to the standard BN1 or BN2 specifications ruling at the time. There were no special body or mechanical specification derivatives built on the production line, except for certain examples with special colour schemes which were usually for show purpose, such as the pink and black cars created for the 1955 London Motor Show.

A wide selection of extra equipment was available from The Donald Healey Motor Company, ranging from hardtops, through extra instrumentation and radios to fitted luggage for the boot.

SPECIFICATION

Type code	Austin-Healey 100, type designation BN1 from 1953 to 1955; BN2 from 1955 to 1956.
Built	Pre-production built at Donald Healey Motor Co. Ltd, Warwick. Volume production at the Longbridge Plant of Austin Motor Company.
Production volume	10,688 BN1; 3924 BN2 (approx 1200 100M derivatives within the BN2 total).
Configuration	Front engine, manual transmission with overdrive and rear wheel drive, open sports type body.

BN1 Series

Engine	Austin-designed four cylinder pushrod OHV unit with watercooled cast iron block and head. Originally used in the Austin A90 Atlantic Convertible Saloon introduced in 1949. Bore 87.3mm (3.4375ins); stroke 111.1mm (4.375ins); displacement 2660cc (162.2cu.in); 7.5 to 1 compression ratio. Maximum power, 90bhp at 4000rpm Maximum torque, 144lb/ft at 2000rpm Two HS4 SU semi-downdraught carburetters with Burgess pancake-type air filters. SU electric high pressure pump mounted on the heel board. 54.6 litre (12 gallon) fuel tank. Lubricating oil capacity 6.68 litres (11.75 Imp. pints). Cooling system capacity 11.37 litres (20 Imp. pints) pressurised to 7psi. Running temperature 75°C to 80°C (190°F).

Clutch	Borg and Beck single dry plate clutch, 23cms (9″) diameter. Mechanical actuation.
Gearbox	Three forward ratios (synchromesh engagement) and reverse, with overdrive on the top two forward ratios. Main gearbox controlled by floor-mounted gearlever. Overdrive operation electrically controlled by fascia panel switch, to give a choice of five forward gear ratios. Oil capacity 2.56 litres (4.5 Imp. pints). Ratios: 1st 2.24; 2nd 1.42; 3rd 1.00; reverse 4.97; overdrive 0.756 (32%) to Chassis 140204, then 0.778 (28%).
Rear axle	To Chassis 221535, spiral bevel three-quarter floating type with 4.125 ratio. Alternative 3.66 to 1 ratio available. Oil capacity 1.42 litres (2.5 Imp. pints). From Chassis 221536 onwards, hypoid bevel three-quarter floating type with 4.10 ratio. Oil capacity 1.70 litres (3.0 Imp. pints).
Overall gear ratios	Direct drive on 4.125 axle: 1st gear 9.28; 2nd gear 5.85; top gear 4.125. With 32% overdrive engaged: 2nd gear 4.42; top gear 3.12. With 28% overdrive engaged: 2nd gear 4.56; top gear 3.28. Reverse gear ratio, 20.5. Direct drive on 4.10 axle: 1st gear 9.22; 2nd gear 5.82; top gear 4.10. With 28% overdrive engaged: 2nd gear 4.52; top gear 3.18. Reverse gear ratio, 20.4.
Road speeds at 1000rpm engine speed	Top gear with 4.125 axle, 17.9mph. 32% Overdrive top gear with 4.125 axle, 24.5mph. 28% Overdrive top gear with 4.125 axle, 24.1mph. Top gear with 4.10 axle, 18.1mph. 28% Overdrive top gear with 4.10 axle, 23.2mph.
Steering	Burman cam and peg steering gear. Three piece track rod. Steering ratio 12.6 to 1. Steering Wheel diameter, 16.5 in. Turning circle, 35 feet diameter.
Suspension: Front Rear	Independent by double wishbone arms and coil springs, controlled by Armstrong double action lever-arm dampers functioning as the top suspension link. Anti-rollbar cross connection. Semi-elliptic leaf springs, controlled by double action Armstrong lever hydraulic dampers. Panhard rod for lateral control.
Brakes	Girling hydraulic 11 inch diameter drum brake system with two leading shoes at the front. Shoe width 1.75in front and rear until Chassis 221536 when rear shoes increased in width to 2.25in. Cable operated handbrake to the rear wheels.
Wheels and tyres	48 spoke centre lock wirewheels with 15 x 4$^{1}/_{2}$ J rim. 5.90 x 15 Dunlop Road Speed tyres as standard specification. 165/15 radial ply tyres as current equivalent. Pressures : Front 20psi, Rear 23psi.

Chassis	Box section longitudinal sidemembers with cruciform centre section cross bracing, and front and rear crossmembers. Integral welded body framing.
Electrical system	12 volt positive earth system. Two six volt batteries of 50 amp. hour capacity at 10 hour rate. Lucas C45 Dynamo. Lucas M418G Starter. Lucas RB 106 Regulator. Lucas SF6 Fuse Unit. Lucas CRT 15 Windscreen Wiper system. Twin Lucas Altette horns. Lucas F700 Headlamps with 42/36 watt prefocus bulbs for RHD cars. For LHD cars Lucas type number 301 36/36 watt prefocus bulbs. Master switch to isolate electrical system located in boot space.
Bodywork	Open 2-seat-style flush panelled coachwork. Full all-weather protection with folding hood and detachable side screens. Full length tonneau cover. Fold flat windscreen. Aluminium body centre sections with bolt-on steel wings to facilitate accident repairs. Connolly leather facings to twin bucket seats. Leather trimmed cushion on transmission tunnel.

Main dimensions and weight		
	Overall length	3.83m (12ft 7in).
	Overall width	1.54m (5ft 0$\frac{1}{2}$in).
	Height over scuttle	0.90m (2ft 11$\frac{1}{2}$in).
	Height over hood	1.24m (4ft 1in).
	Wheelbase	2.29m (7ft 6in).
	Front track	1.24m (4ft 1in).
	Rear track	1.29m (4ft 2$\frac{3}{4}$in).
	Ground clearance	0.14m (5$\frac{1}{2}$in).
	Kerb weight	987kg (2176lb).

BN2 Series

Specification generally as BN1 except –

Gearbox	Four forward speed ratios and reverse. Synchromesh engagement on second, third and top gear ratios. Short, floor-mounted gearlever. Overdrive on the top two forward ratios, electrically controlled from fascia-mounted switch to give a choice of six forward gears. Oil capacity 2.98 litres (5.25 Imp. pints).
Ratios	1st 3.07; 2nd 1.91; 3rd 1.33; 4th 1.00; reverse 4.17; overdrive ratio 0.778
Overall gear ratios	Direct drive: 12.60; 7.85; 5.46; 4.10; forward, and 17.10 reverse. Overdrive ratios: 4.24 and 3.18 on third and top gear, respectively.
Road speeds at 1000rpm engine speed	Top gear with 4.10 axle ratio, 18.1mph. Overdrive top gear with 4.10 axle ratio, 23.2mph.
Suspension	Revised rate and increased travel front springs. Taper roller front wheel hub bearings.

Brakes	Front brake shoes increased in width to 2.25in.
Electrical	Self-parking Lucas DR2 windscreen wiper system.
Bodywork	Front wheel opening cut line raised by 1.25in to allow full bump clearance with revised suspension travel. On late cars, the body's side crease line is carried through past the back wheel opening to the rear of the panel.

100M model

Specification generally as BN2 with the following revisions –

Engine	8.1 to 1 compression ratio; high lift, extended period camshaft; twin $1^3/_4$ inch H6 SU carburetter on revised inlet manifold; modified distributor ignition advance curve. Maximum power, 110bhp at 4500rpm. Maximum torque, 144lb/ft at 2000rpm with extended range when compared with the standard engine.
Suspension	Stiffer, larger diameter front anti-roll bar.
Bodywork	Louvred bonnet with Le Mans regulation bonnet strap. Two tone paint finish in a variety of colours.

Special Tuning Kit, for standard BN1 and BN2 models

A "Le Mans" engine modification kit, Part Number P280, suitable for fitting to standard specification BN1 and BN2 cars giving a substantial performance increase. With standard 7.5 to 1 compression pistons, engine output was raised to 100bhp at 4500rpm. In combination with 8.1 to 1 compression pistons as fitted to the 100M output rose to 110bhp at 4500rpm. Additional special tuning parts for the serious competition driver were: aero screens; larger capacity fuel tanks of 15 or 25 Imp. gallons capacity; Alfin brake drums; close ratio (22%) overdrive unit; 100M anti-roll bar; high ratio 3.66 to 1 crownwheel and pinion assembly together with revised calibration speedometer to suit; special race type silencer.

All parts were available for either after-market dealer fitting or for owner fitting as required by the customer, or for fitting by the Donald Healey Motor Company to new car orders.

Accessories, all models

A comprehensive range of accessories embracing woodrim steering wheels, additional driving lamps, two styles of hardtop, radios, additional instruments, boot-mounted luggage racks, fitted suitcases and chromium plated cylinder rocker covers was available from the Donald Healey Motor Co. It was also possible to have the fascia panel and cockpit trim rails covered with leather cloth to match the interior trim colour.

Performance (hood and side screen erected)

	BN1	BN2 (100M)
Advertised bhp	90 at 4000rpm	110 at 4500rpm
Max. speed (mph)	102*	109*
Acceleration (seconds):		
0 – 30mph	4.0	3.4
0 – 60mph	11.7	9.6
0 – 90mph	27.4	24.3
Standing start 1/4 mile (sec)	18.1	17.4

Lowering the weather equipment and folding the windscreen into the racing position raises the maximum speed by 5 to 8mph.

ROAD TESTS

AUTOSPORT, OCTOBER 24, 1952

TIMED SECTION: The Healey "Hundred" flashing over the measured mile on the Jabbeke-Aeltre motor-road.

stiffening, and particular attention has been given to the easy replacement of individual panels in the event of an accident. Although the upper works are of aluminium, the side sections are of sheet steel to provide greater resistance to minor bruising.

The front suspension is by wishbones and coil springs, a new departure for this make, as trailing arms have always been favoured. Behind, a normal spiral bevel axle rests on semi-elliptic springs. As the two-seater body is very low, a deep shaft tunnel also encloses the gearbox. Development work has shown that weight distribution is vital to good roadholding, and the optimum result is achieved with the rear wheels rather more heavily laden than the front.

The engine is an Austin A.90, of 2,660 c.c. It gives 90 b.h.p. at 4,000 r.p.m. but, of even greater importance, it has an unusually flat power curve. It is a normal pushrod unit of modern design, and naturally spares and service facilities are available everywhere. The Austin gear-

JOHN BOLSTER TESTS—

The HEALEY "HUNDRED"

An entirely new Medium-priced British Sports-car with excellent Power-weight Ratio and capable of over 105 m.p.h.—A certain Dollar-earner

AMONG the manufacturers of sports-cars, the name of Healey is an enviable one. Founded by a famous competition driver, the firm has produced nothing but speed models since its inception. Consequently, the introduction of an entirely new Healey is an event of great importance in the motoring world.

The object of the new model can be simply stated. It is a very fast everyday road car, of superior refinement and with exceptionally fine handling qualities. It has a simple push-rod engine that has not been tuned in any way, and which is consequently easy to service and gives its full power on pool petrol. The admittedly excellent performance is due entirely to low weight and an efficient aerodynamic shape. It is

purely incidental that, in following this formula, Donald Healey has produced by far the cheapest fully-equipped car that will exceed a genuine, timed - both - ways 100 m.p.h.

Compact Dimensions

If you are going to build a light car, the first essential is to keep the overall dimensions small. Thus, a wheelbase of 7 ft. 6 ins. has been chosen, which, with a front track of 4 ft. 0¾ in. and a rear track of 4 ft. 1½ ins., ensures a compact vehicle. The basis of the main structure is a pair of box-section side members, which run the full length of the car, and pass beneath the rear axle. They are united by cruciform bracing, also of box section. The body and undershield provide additional

box is also used, operated by a short, central lever.

Behind the gearbox is a Laycock De Normanville overdrive unit. As is proper for a car of this type, the change is manual, through a short lever mounted on the shaft tunnel to the rear of the main control. The actual selection is electrical, and the step-up ratio is 0.756 to 1. If an overdrive is not specified, a 3.66 to 1 final drive replaces the usual 4.125 ratio.

Try-Out at Jabbeke

As the car became available while I was in Paris, for the Salon and kindred activities, it was decided that a Continental road test would be advantageous. Accordingly, Donald Healey and his son met me at Ostend, with the famous Jabbeke

Super Profile

AUTOSPORT, OCTOBER 24, 1952

motor road very much in mind. My first impression, as I drove out of the town, was that the engine was astonishingly flexible. With so little weight to pull, it has complete mastery of any situation, and the acceleration on the direct drive is brisk from even a crawl.

The steering is quite remarkably light at all speeds, and although it does not feel "dead", there is no objectionable return motion. Road noises are not apparent, even on Belgian *pavé*, a considerable achievement with an all-enveloping body. The town and traffic manners are in fact beyond reproach, and the good visibility is appreciated under such conditions.

On arrival at the Jabbeke straight,

GOOD-LOOKER : With hood erected, the Healey still retains a simple beauty of line which is essentially modern.

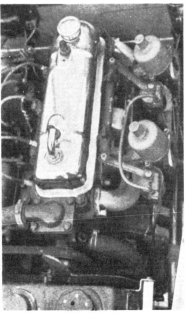

PERFECTLY STANDARD: (Above) The A.90 Austin engine as used on the "Hundred" is a normal production unit.

★

OVER THE "TON": (Right) The Healey travelling at over 100 m.p.h. on the famous Belgian motor-road.

the Editor and two stop watches occupied the passenger's seat. We decided to time for maximum speed over the measured mile that is used for record attempts, and of course we took the mean of runs in both directions. As will be seen from the data panel, an average of 106 m.p.h. was achieved, with which we were more than pleased. Since the road was not closed at the time, heavy traffic, and even a herd of cows, rendered our task a difficult one. As a result, quite a mileage was put in at over 100 m.p.h., without any sign of stress.

During the timed runs, the rev.-counter remained steady at 4,250 r.p.m. On the gears, about 4,800 r.p.m. can be attained before obvious valve bounce sets in. I would guess that the actual power peak lies rather below 4,500 r.p.m., however.

With such an advantageous power/weight ratio, first speed is purely an emergency gear. Even for the standing start acceleration figures, second was used for the getaway, but no time was lost thereby, as the results prove. Rearward weight distribution, and a light axle, give exceptional freedom from wheelspin, while slight juddering can only be produced by the most merciless misuse of the clutch. The latter component is well up to its work, and takes no exception to repeated racing starts.

Freedom from Roll

The suspension is first class, and one is at no time conscious of the short wheelbase. I have not watched this car being cornered fast by another driver, but from behind the wheel there is no apparent roll under even the most extreme con-

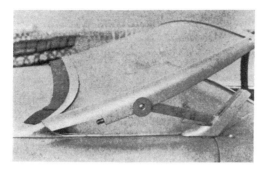

The clever method of folding the windscreen to form a "scuttle". Hinges are secured by thumbscrews.

★

★

The Healey "Hundred"—*continued*
ditions. Such freedom from rolling usually goes only with hard suspension, and one assumes that an extra low centre of gravity is responsible for this happy state of affairs.

A balance has been struck whereby neither understeering nor oversteering is favoured. There must be just enough understeer to promote stability, for the car travels straight and true at high speeds without any conscious guidance. It is very much at home on fast bends, and a four-wheel drift can be held if desired. The steering is fairly low geared, but as the rear end never breaks away unexpectedly, this is a matter of no moment.

My first impression of the brakes was that they were not particularly powerful, but this was soon proved to be erroneous. The initial pressure on the pedal, for moderately quick stops, is rather more than is normal these days, but thereafter the retardation is progressive. I had occasion to brake hard from three-figure speeds quite frequently, but no fading was apparent, and the car remained steady.

All the controls are well placed, and only the overdrive requires comment. One can change on full throttle, either up or down; in fact the smoothest engagement is secured in this way. The wide two-seater body gives good protection. One sits well down in it, and there is a neat hood. An ingenious folding screen can be slid forward and secured in sockets on the scuttle. There is a fair-sized luggage boot in the tail.

Flexibility at Low Speeds

I concluded my test by getting off the main roads, and sampling some Belgian by-ways. Cobbled village streets, dirt roads, and even farm tracks, were all on the menu, but the Healey took them in its stride. One can use the direct drive down almost to walking pace under such conditions, and it was difficult to imagine that this was the car that I had just been driving at 106 m.p.h.

Back on the main highway, I was soon up to a quiet, effortless 90 m.p.h. cruising speed again, with "the ton" available on any reasonable straight. Except for a healthy

AUTOSPORT, OCTOBER 24, 1952

boom from the exhaust, this is a car that makes little noise, and whether the engine is fundamentally silent or the sound-proofing particularly effective, it certainly adds to the pleasure of driving.

A genuine sports-car should provide exceptional performance and stamina, coupled with a very high degree of controllability. The new Healey has these qualities in abundance, and in addition it shatters all previous concepts of value for money in this field. With its lightly stressed and easily serviced engine, it should stand up to a long life of hard driving. This is certainly the most important new model that we have seen for some time.

SPECIFICATION AND PERFORMANCE DATA

Car Tested: Healey "Hundred" Two-seater. Price £850 plus £473 14s. 5d. P.T. In U.S.A. (N.Y.) $3,000. (Overdrive extra.)

Engine: Four cylinders, 87.3 mm. x 111.1 mm. (2,660 c.c.). 7.5 to 1 compression ratio. 90 b.h.p. at 4,000 r.p.m. Pushrod operated o.h.v. Two S.U. carburetters. Lucas coil and distributor ignition with vacuum and centrifugal advance.

Transmission: Four-speed synchromesh gearbox with Laycock-De Normanville overdrive, ratios 14.8, 9.3, 5.85, 4.125 (direct), and 3.12 (overdrive) to 1.

Chassis: Integral body and frame construction, based on parallel box-section side members with cruciform box-section bracing. Independent front suspension by wishbones and coil springs, with Girling hydraulic dampers incorporated in the top links. Burman steering gear with three-piece track rod and slave arm. Front anti-roll bar. Spiral bevel rear axle suspended on semi-elliptic springs, with lateral location by Panhard rod. Girling 2-L.S. hydraulic brakes in 10 in. drums. 5.50 in. x 16 in. tyres on perforated disc wheels (wire wheels extra).

Equipment: 12 volt lighting and starting. Speedometer, rev. counter, ammeter, oil pressure and water-temperature gauges.

Dimensions: Wheelbase, 7 ft. 6 ins. Track, 4 ft. 0¾ in. front, 4 ft. 1½ ins. rear. Weight, 16 cwt. 3 qrs. Turning circle, 30 ft.

Performance: Maximum speed, 106.05 m.p.h. (170.9 k.p.h.). Speeds in gears, fourth (direct), 92 m.p.h., third, 65 m.p.h., second, 40.5 m.p.h. **Acceleration:** Standing quarter-mile, 18 secs., standing kilometre, 33.95 secs.; 0-50 m.p.h., 8.5 secs., 0-60 m.p.h., 10.5 secs., 0-70 m.p.h., 15 secs., 0-80 m.p.h., 20 secs., 0-90 m.p.h., 26 secs., 0-100 m.p.h., 37.2 secs.

Fuel Consumption: 25 m.p.g.

Three-quarter rear view of the handsome and effective 2.7-litre Healey "Hundred"

October 29, 1952.

The **Motor**

LOW DRAG is achieved on the new Healey by very clean body lines plus, optionally, a smooth undershield. Note how the windscreen may be tilted back to form a wind deflector. The two separate seats are shaped to give comfort and support, the gear-lever being set centrally on the transmission hump.

1953 CARS
The
AUSTIN-HEALEY HUNDRED
Full Details of New A 90-engined Model
Introduced on Show Opening Day

ONE of the most attractive sports cars exhibited at Earls Court is the new Austin-Healey Hundred, which appeared at the Show as a last-minute surprise. This new model is interesting, both in itself and for the fact that it is an entirely new design quite unlike other Healey models. Powered by an A90 engine, complete with clutch and gearbox, it has coil-and-wishbone front suspension, an immensely sturdy and very low-built chassis frame fabricated from rectangular and square-section steel tubes, and is fitted with an extremely attractive two-seater body. Intended primarily as an export model, it sells for a basic price of £850 (or, with purchase tax in Britain, for a total figure of £1,323 14s. 5d.).

*　　*　　*

The well-tried Austin A90 engine, with its power output of 90 b.h.p. at 4,000 r.p.m., is already familiar to readers of "The Motor." The standard clutch and gearbox are used but a Laycock-de Normanville overdrive is available as an extra. When it is fitted, an axle ratio of 4.125 to 1 is employed, which gives an overdrive top of 3.12; without the overdrive, a higher axle ratio of 3.66 is used, this also giving a high third of 5.19 to 1.

The overdrive fits neatly at the back of the existing gearbox and thence an unusually short propeller shaft leads to a conventional back axle, which passes over the underslung rear portion of the frame and is located laterally by a Panhard rod, thus relieving the springs of this function. Reverting to the gearbox, changes are effected by a neat, centrally placed, remote-control lever.

Basis of the chassis frame is a pair of 3-in. by 3-in.-section steel tubes, which are, in fact, fabricated from two channel-section halves welded together, a form of construction which has advantages in that accurate control of the thickness of material is easier than in the case of extruded tubes. These main longerons are comparatively close together and, with

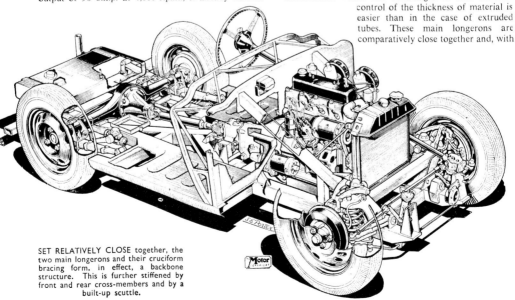

SET RELATIVELY CLOSE together, the two main longerons and their cruciform bracing form, in effect, a backbone structure. This is further stiffened by front and rear cross-members and by a built-up scuttle.

The Motor | October 29, 1952.

The Austin-Healey Hundred - - Contd.

a cruciform structure in the centre, form, in effect, a central backbone.

At the front, a fabricated cross-member embodying 3-in. and 2-in. square tubes superimposed, forms a very rigid mounting for the suspension units. This cross-member is further braced (again by rectangular tubes) to a built-up scuttle member consisting of a pair of channel-section hoops cross-braced by light diagonal angle-section struts rather reminiscent of aircraft construction; to this structure is welded a bulkhead embodying foot ramps for the body.

At the rear of the chassis, a further rectangular tube is welded to the ends of the main longerons and extended laterally to provide mounting for the shackles of the rear semi-elliptic springs, the forward ends of the springs being attached to outriggers of the same construction as the rest of the frame. The portion between the scuttle structure and the forward spring outriggers is enclosed by welded-steel floorboards, given additional support at their outer edges by angle-section members. The net result is a frame of moderate weight, very low build and exceptional torsional rigidity.

As will have been gathered, the semi-elliptic rear springs are located outside the main frame members, at a considerable distance but parallel to them. Control is by double-acting Girling dampers bolted to the main longerons. Similar dampers, but built in to the upper suspension links, are used at the front, where the i.f.s. is of unequal-wishbone type. An anti-roll bar is used.

Burman steering is employed, with the steering box mounted on a bracket on the front extremity of the main frame on one side, a similar bracket on the other carrying an idler member for the three-piece track rod, the whole arrangement designed both to eliminate steering interference by wheel movement and to provide for right or left-hand steering with equal ease.

Other chassis features of interest include Girling hydraulic brakes with two-leading shoes at the front, pierced disc wheels (knock-on wire type as an optional extra) and a very squat rear tank holding 10½ gallons.

The clean design of the under part of the frame

PIERCED DISC wheels, grouped instruments and the smooth body contours are notable here. The externally-accessible boot is commendably roomy for a car of this type. Knock-on wire wheels are obtainable if required.

(coupled with the fact that the rear axle and transmission line generally pass above it), permits an unusually smooth undershield to be fitted (as an extra, if desired), this undershield being entirely clear of any excrescences or apertures from the sump to the rear extremity of the car where it meets the body.

Although intended as a two-seater (the transmission line is an obstacle to three-abreast seating on such a low-built car), the body is notably wide, with an internal measurement between the front-hinged doors of 50 ins.

The facia board is cut away on the passenger's side and the compact instrument panel in front of the driver carries a rev. counter and speedometer (both with 4-in. dials), together with a fuel gauge, and combined oil-pressure gauge and thermometer.

The large single-piece windscreen is mounted on pillars incorporating swinging links so arranged that, when desired, the entire screen can be swung forward at the base and simultaneously tilted back at the top to form a wind deflector—a most sensible alternative to the usual fold-flat arrangement. The hood disappears behind the seats when furled and has a large rear window of flexible plastic. Side screens are of frameless Perspex and pegged into the doors.

A top-hinged panel gives access to a boot which also houses the spare wheel and the filler for the rear tank. Other items of note include a bonnet aperture with rear-hinged panel, bumpers (with over-riders) front and rear, built-in long-range head lamps, separate side lamps, twin wipers and a spring-spoke steering wheel.

AUSTIN-HEALEY HUNDRED DATA

Engine Dimensions :		Engine Details—Contd.		Chassis Details—Contd.	
Cylinders ..	4	Battery capacity ..	63 amp/hrs	Wheel type ..	Disc (optional, knock-on wire)
Bore	87.3 mm.			Tyre size	5.50 - 16 (5.90 - 15 with
Stroke	111.1 mm.	**Transmission :**			wire wheels)
Cubic capacity ..	2660 c.c.	Clutch	10-in. Borg and Beck	Steering gear ..	Burman
Piston area ..	37.2 sq. in.		s.d.p.	Steering wheel ..	16-in.
Valves	o.h.v. (push-rod)	Gear ratios : Top ..	Standard 3.66		
Compression ratio	7.5 to 1		With overdrive 4.125	**Dimensions :**	
			(overdrive 3.12)	Wheelbase	7 ft. 6 ins.
Engine Performance :		3rd ..	Standard 5.19	Track : Front ..	4 ft. 0½ ins.
Max. b.h.p. ..	90		(with overdrive 5.85)	Rear ..	4 ft. 1½ ins.
at	4000 r.p.m.	2nd ..	Standard 8.23	Overall length ..	12 ft. 2 ins.
Max. b.m.e.p. ..	134 lb/sq in,		(with overdrive 9.30)	Overall width ..	5 ft.
at	2000 r.p.m.	1st	Standard 13.18	Overall height ..	3 ft 11 ins. (hood up
B.H.P. per sq. in. piston			with overdrive 14.85)		4 ft. 1 in.)
area	2.42	Rev. ..	Standard 20.6	Ground clearance ..	7 ins.
Peak piston speed ft. per			(with overdrive 28.25)	Turning Circle ..	30 ft.
min.	2930	Prop. shaft ..	Hardy Spicer open	Dry weight	16¾ cwt.
		Final drive ..	Spiral bevel		
Engine Details :				**Performance Data :**	
Carburetter ..	2 S.U. horizontal			Piston area, sq. in. per	
Ignition	Coil	**Chassis Details :**		ton	44.4
Plugs : make and type ..	Champion NA8	Brakes	Girling hydraulic (2LS on	Brake lining area, sq. in.	
Fuel Pump ..	AC Mechanical		front)	per ton	158
Fuel capacity ..	10½ gallons.	Brake drum diameter ..	10 ins.	*Top gear m.p.h. per	
Oil filter	Suction gauze	Friction lining area ..	132.2 sq. ins.	1,000 r.p.m. ..	Standard 21.1
Oil capacity ..	13 pints.	Suspension : Front ..	Independent (coil and		Overdrive 24.7
Cooling system ..	Pump, fan and thermo-		wishbone)	*Top gear m.p.h. at 2,500	
	stat			ft./min. piston speed ..	Standard 72.5
Water capacity ..	19 pints	Rear ..	Semi-elliptic		Overdrive 85.2
Electrical system..	12-volt	Shock absorbers ..	Girling hydraulic	*Litres per ton-mile dry ..	Standard, 4530
					Overdrive, 3860

* Figures given are with standard 5.50-16 tyres.

September 16, 1953.

The Motor Continental Road Test No. 7C/53—

Make : Austin-Healey **Type :** "Hundred"

Makers : Austin Motor Co. Ltd., Longbridge, Birmingham

Dimensions and Seating

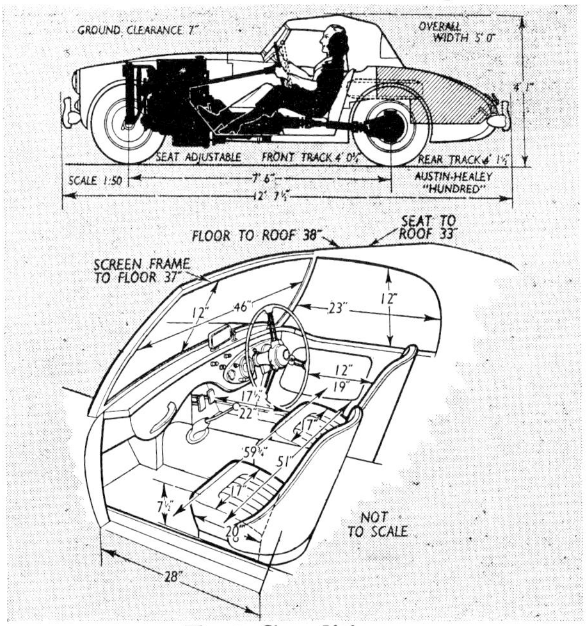
GROUND CLEARANCE 7"
OVERALL WIDTH 5' 0"
4' 1"
SEAT ADJUSTABLE
FRONT TRACK 4' 0¾"
REAR TRACK 4' 1½"
SCALE 1:50
7' 6"
12' 7½"
AUSTIN-HEALEY "HUNDRED"
FLOOR TO ROOF 38"
SEAT TO ROOF 33"
SCREEN FRAME TO FLOOR 37"
12"
46"
23"
12"
12"
19"
17½"
22"
17"
59¾"
51"
7½"
17"
20"
NOT TO SCALE
28"

Test Conditions

Hot, dry weather, with slight cross wind. Dry concrete surface (Ostend-Ghent Motor Road). Premium grade fuel. Hood and sidescreens erect except for certain maximum speed runs.

Test Data

ACCELERATION TIMES on Three Upper Ratios

	Overdrive top	Direct top	2nd
10-30 m.p.h.	—	6.6 sec.	3.8 sec.
20-40 m.p.h.	—	6.5 sec.	[illegible].9 sec.
30-50 m.p.h.	—	6.3 sec.	3.9 sec.
40-60 m.p.h.	8.7 sec.	6.2 sec.	4.5 sec.
50-70 m.p.h.	8.7 sec.	6.7 sec.	—
60-80 m.p.h.	11.7 sec.	9.4 sec.	—
70-90 m.p.h.	13.5 sec.	11.2 sec.	—

ACCELERATION TIMES Through Gears

0-30 m.p.h.	3.8 sec.
0-40 m.p.h.	6.1 sec.
0-50 m.p.h.	8.5 sec.
0-60 m.p.h.	11.2 sec.
0-70 m.p.h.	15.8 sec.
0-80 m.p.h.	21.1 sec.
0-90 m.p.h.	28.2 sec.
Standing Quarter Mile	18.5 sec.

FUEL CONSUMPTION

36.5 m.p.g. at constant 30 m.p.h.*
39.5 m.p.g. at constant 40 m.p.h.
34.0 m.p.g. at constant 50 m.p.h.
32.0 m.p.g. at constant 60 m.p.h.
27.5 m.p.g. at constant 70 m.p.h.
22.0 m.p.g. at constant 80 m.p.h.
20.0 m.p.g. at constant 90 m.p.h.
Overall consumption for 871 miles, 38.7 gallons, = 22.5 m.p.g.

* Direct top.

MAXIMUM SPEEDS

Flying Half Mile (Windscreen folded down)

Mean of four opposite runs .. 106.0 m.p.h.
Best time equals .. .. 107.2 m.p.h.

(Hood and sidescreens erect)

Mean of two opposite runs .. 101.5 m.p.h.

Speed in Gears

Max. speed in direct top .. 90 m.p.h.
Max. speed in direct 2nd gear .. 60 m.p.h.
Max. speed in 1st gear .. .. 35 m.p.h.

WEIGHT

Unladen kerb weight	18½ cwt.
Front/rear weight distribution	51/49
Weight laden as tested	22 cwt.

INSTRUMENTS

Speedometer at 30 m.p.h.	accurate
Speedometer at 60 m.p.h.	accurate
Speedometer at 90 m.p.h.	2% slow
Distance recorder	accurate

HILL CLIMBING (At steady speeds)

	Overdrive top	Direct top
Max. speed on 1 in 20	90 m.p.h.	90 m.p.h.
Max. speed on 1 in 15	84 m.p.h.	89 m.p.h.
Max. speed on 1 in 10	70 m.p.h.	80 m.p.h.
Max. gradient on overdrive top gear	1 in 8.9	(Tapley 250 lb/ton)
Max. gradient on direct top gear	1 in 6.9	(Tapley 320 lb/ton)
Max. gradient on 2nd gear	1 in 4.4	(Tapley 495 lb/ton)

BRAKES at 30 m.p.h.

0.85 g retardation (= 35½ ft. stopping distance) with 110 lb. pedal pressure
0.82 g retardation (= 36½ ft. stopping distance) with 75 lb. pedal pressure
0.45 g retardation (= 67 ft. stopping distance) with 50 lb. pedal pressure
0.21 g retardation (=143 ft. stopping distance) with 25 lb. pedal pressure

In Brief

Price £750 plus purchase tax £313 12 6 equals £1,063 12 6.

Capacity	2,660 c.c.
Unladen kerb weight	18½ cwt.
Fuel consumption	22.5 m.p.g.
Maximum speed	106.0 m.p.h.
Maximum speed on 1 in 20 gradient	90 m.p.h.
Maximum direct top gear gradient	1 in 6.9

Acceleration:
10-30 m.p.h in direct top .. 6.6 sec.
0-50 m.p.h. through gears .. 8.5 sec.

Gearing (overdrive figures in brackets): 21.0 (27.8) m.p.h in top at 1,000 r.p.m. 72.0 (95.2) m.p.h. at 2,500 ft. per min. piston speed.

Specification

Engine

Cylinders	4
Bore	87.3 mm.
Stroke	111.1 mm.
Cubic Capacity	2,660 c.c.
Piston area	37.2 sq. in.
Valves	Overhead (push rod)
Compression ratio	7.5/1
Max. power	90 b.h.p.
at	4,000 r.p.m.
Piston speed at max. b.h.p.	2,920 ft. per min.
Carburetters	2 S.U. horizontal
Ignition	Coil
Sparking Plugs	Champion NA8
Fuel Pump	S.U. Electric
Oil filter	Suction gauze

Transmission

Clutch	10-in. Borg & Beck s.d.p.
Overdrive top gear (electric)	2.775
Top gear (s/m)	3.667
Overdrive 2nd gear (electric)	3.84
2nd gear (s/m)	5.08
1st gear (s/m)	9.05
Propeller shaft	Hardy Spicer, open
Final drive	Spiral bevel

Chassis

Brakes	Girling hydraulic (2LS front)
Brake drum diameter	11 in.
Friction lining area	145.2 sq. in.
Suspension: Front	Coil and wishbone i.f.s.
Rear	Semi-elliptic
Shock absorbers	Girling hydraulic
Tyres	5.90-15

Steering

Steering gear	Burman cam and lever
Turning circle	30 ft.
Turns of steering wheel, lock to lock	2½

Performance factors: (at laden weight as tested)

Piston area, sq. in. per ton	33.8
Brake lining area, sq. in. per ton	132
Specific displacement, litres per ton mile, Overdrive top	2,610
Direct top	3,455

Fully described in "The Motor," October 29, 1952.

Maintenance

Fuel tank: 12 gallons. **Sump:** 11¾ pints, S.A.E. 30. **Gearbox:** 5½ pints, S.A.E. 40. **Rear axle:** 2½ pints, E.P. 140. **Steering gear:** E.P.140 gear oil. **Radiator:** 19 pints (2 drain taps). **Chassis lubrication:** By grease gun every 500 miles to 7 points, every 2,000 miles to 14 further points. **Ignition timing:** 6° B.T.D.C., static. **Spark plug gap:** 0.025 in. **Contact breaker gap:** 0.012 in. **Valve timing:** I. O., 5° B.T.D.C.; I. C., 45° A.B.D.C.; E. O., 40° B.B.D.C.; E. C., 10° A.T.D.C. **Tappet clearances:** (Cold), Inlet 0.015 in., Exhaust 0.015 in. **Front wheel toe-in:** $\frac{1}{16}$-$\frac{1}{8}$ in. **Camber angle:** +1°. **Castor angle:** +1¾°. **Tyre pressures:** Front 22 lb., Rear 24 lb. **Brake fluid:** Girling. **Batteries:** Two 6-volt batteries in series, capacity 63 amp. hr. **Lamp bulbs:** 12 volt, headlamps 42/36 watt, tail/stop 6/24 watt, sidelamps 6/18 watt.

Ref. B/27/53.

September 16, 1953.

The Motor

The AUSTIN-HEALEY "HUNDRED"

Exceptional Performance and Economy from a Competitively-priced Sports Two-seater

All-weather comfort or stripped for action. The Austin-Healey is comfortable and easy to see out of whether the hood and sidescreens are raised or the windscreen lowered to act as a wind deflector.

THE announcement in July of this year that the basic price of the Austin-Healey "Hundred," now coming off the assembly line at Longbridge at the rate of 120 a week, had been reduced by £100 to £750, placed a very fast and roadworthy sports car in a price group usually associated with much more sober vehicles. This reduction was made possible by the decision, made soon after the appearance of the Healey at the 1952 Motor Show, that the whole car should be built by the Austin Motor Co.

The car which we were recently able to test differed slightly from those in current production by the use of a gearbox notable for robustness rather than refinement, and of a higher final-drive ratio, which were adopted for the 24-hour race at Le Mans. Some further explanation is necessary of the more than usually comprehensive data given on the opposite page, which results from the fitting as standard equipment of a Laycock-de Normanville overdrive. This transmission, operated by a small switch on one of the steering-wheel spokes, provides a step-up ratio of 1.322:1.

On the test car the overdrive could be used on all three forward speeds, although on production models it is restricted to second and top gears, and in fact only very limited use was possible in bottom gear since the cutting-in speed of about 35 m.p.h. corresponded to the maximum revs. which could humanely be obtained in the indirect gears. With a limit to engine speed dictated by common sense the actual speeds obtainable were 35 m.p.h., 60 m.p.h. and 90 m.p.h. in the normal range, and 42 m.p.h., 70 m.p.h. and the maximum with overdrive engaged, so that a strict progression through the gears would involve a change from overdrive second to direct top. However, common sense again suggested that a more useful indication of get-away would be given without the use of overdrive, and the figures for acceleration through the gears are therefore only for the normal range.

In overdrive the Healey is entirely flexible and, as the Tapley meter shows, no mean performer on even quite steep main-road gradients. At any speed up to 90 m.p.h. still greater acceleration can be had with direct top by flicking the steering-wheel switch and kicking down the accelerator pedal so that when coming up behind another fast car a suitable overtaking ratio can in effect be preselected. The same, of course, applies at lesser speeds in second gear. If the car is allowed to slow below 30 m.p.h. in overdrive, either in gear or in neutral, the next acceleration automatically selects direct drive until this speed is again exceeded.

Inherent Economy

The road speed, in overdrive top, was 27.8 m.p.h. per 1,000 r.p.m. on the car supplied, a fact which no doubt helped to produce the quite remarkable fuel consumption figures. Nevertheless, the gearing of the standard model is also unusually high, giving a speed of 23.8 m.p.h. per 1,000 r.p.m., and the inherent economy of the combination of a light car and the Austin engine, with its Weslake-designed cylinder head, is evident from the overall fuel consumption of 22.5 m.p.g.

It will be clear from these remarks that the Austin-Healey is meant for fast motoring, yet any impression of limited usefulness for other purposes would be quite false. It is a measure of the adaptability of this modern idea of a sports car that drivers who normally go about their business in 8 and 10 horse-

The cockpit and controls need no explanation, except for the overdrive switch on the steering wheel which on production cars is removed to the centre of the facia panel. The rest is in the classic sports-car tradition.

The Motor

September 16, 1953.

The Austin-Healey 100 - - - - - - - Contd.

power saloons can gain their first experience of it quite comfortably in the London rush-hour, or take it straight out on a by-pass and touch 90 m.p.h. with no more alarming effects than a sense of great exhilaration. Certainly it is a sports car, in the best meaning of the phrase; the only adverse qualities from the point of view of everyday motoring are a moderately strident exhaust note, the rather light construction of the bodywork and doors, and a lack of heat insulation between engine compartment and cockpit. At present, the two-bladed fan seems on the small side and the passage for hot air to escape from under the bonnet inadequate, so that in town driving at least there is a tendency for both the engine and the space around the passenger's legs to get too warm.

These things apart, the car can quite well earn its keep for the man who needs no more than two places—two very generous places one may add, for the internal width is 50 in.—and a corresponding space for luggage. It will "potter" if need be, to such an extent that accelerating from 10 m.p.h. in top gear during the test was a pleasanter process than on many family cars, both large and small. The usual rib-chilling slipstream that goes with the older type of open car in cool weather is avoided by seats placed so low within the body that the door tops are almost at shoulder height. The hood is frankly rather a handful for one person to put up unaided, but once it is in position, and the moulded Perspex sidescreens pegged into the doors, the interior is very snug, and should keep out any degree of foul weather. All-round visibility, which is excellent for a tallish driver, although a shorter owner would probably like the seat raised to give him a really good view over the bonnet and wings, is scarcely affected by the hood, owing to the tall windscreen, and wide rear window of flexible plastic material.

Soft, well-shaped bucket seats provide a commanding driving position which matches the quite outstanding roadworthiness. Here again the Healey has made the best of both the old and the new worlds of car design. Low build and well-planned suspension have practically eliminated roll, although the springing is soft enough to take the sting out of even Belgian pavé in a manner worthy of cars weighing considerably more than 18½ cwt. in road trim. Tyre squeal also is unobtrusive on corners, although some road surfaces bring it on very loudly under braking.

"Alive" Steering

The steering is exceedingly good. Anyone accustomed solely to the familiar "lost-motion" type of modern steering would be astonished at its precision, yet those who expect quickness to be accompanied by heavy operation would be equally surprised. It has a liveliness and delicacy of touch which can be bettered by few cars on the road. There is a nicely judged modicum of under-steer, and all that is necessary is to turn the wheel and hold it there. Pressed to the absolute limit, the car shows a sharp rear-end breakaway, the sturdy rear axle showing a slight tendency to hop on bumps. The 2½ turns lock-to-lock, incidentally, cover a turning circle of only 30 feet, and the steering wheel is adjustable for reach. It is interesting to observe that this neo-vintage quality of steering is found in a car with a front/rear weight distribution of 51/49 unladen, while the weight of luggage, a 12-gallon petrol tank and passengers is all preponderately on the back wheels. Even under standing start acceleration test conditions there was little wheelspin for a car with such a high power-weight ratio.

Driving on many familiar stretches of main road becomes a different art altogether with the Healey. Corners which previously were a test of skill are taken as fast as traffic conditions will allow, so easily as to become almost insignificant. Moreover, even this treatment does not throw either driver or passenger about in the car—an advantage of shaped bucket seats

and lateral stability which is not always appreciated. For a "real" sensation of cornering it is necessary to find open road bends on which to drive faster than the usual family car's cruising speed.

While these comments apply to the dry roads which were found throughout the period of our test, it should be safe to assume that on a wet surface the road-holding would still be very good.

With a friction lining area of 161 sq in. per ton of dry weight, the brakes are extremely powerful for quite light pedal pressures, although an adjustment to put more braking effort on the back wheels might give slightly better results. Several rapid stops in quick succession produced a rather unpleasant judder from the front brakes, and appeared to lower their efficiency.

Instruments and controls on the Austin-Healey are as one would expect on a thoroughbred car, well-placed and nearly comprehensive. Only an ammeter is lacking amongst the former, which include 4-inch rev. counter and speedometer (of unusual accuracy), oil pressure gauge and water thermometer, with warning lights for ignition, high-beam headlamps and overdrive engagement. The pull-up hand brake is most effective. Additional elbow room is provided by large recesses in the doors with a deep pocket at the bottom, but one restriction on the car tested was the inability to make any kind of signal with the hood and sidescreens up. Flashing light direction indicators are however available if required, and the twin horns are powerful.

The headlamps, which admittedly were aimed too high on the test car, were scarcely in keeping with its performance, so that on a fast road 70 m.p.h. was felt to be quite fast enough using only the headlamps, although this could be improved with the use of the Lucas "Flamethrower" fitted as an extra.

Of all the outstanding features of the Austin-Healey perhaps the most attractive is the combination of a simple, robust engine and gearbox with the quick-acting overdrive unit. Intelligent spacing of five forward speeds makes this a most delightful car.

Under-bonnet accessibility is very good. The forward facing cold air intake for the twin carburetters is an optional fitting.

Luggage rests on the flat-topped petrol tank in the boot, the latter being exceptionally large for the type of car.

Road Test:
THE AUSTIN-HEALEY 100-M
improved performance thanks to the "LeMans kit"

Ever since the "LeMans" kit was announced as optional equipment for the Austin-Healey "100," we have been besieged by inquiries—what is included, what is the cost, how much is performance improved, etc.—and some answers are about due.

For 1956, the Austin company have announced a third model for the Healey line-up, the 100-M. For $290 more than the price of a standard 100 model, one gets the following extras, factory installed.

1. An 8.10-to-1 compression ratio obtained by a steel head gasket.
2. A high-lift camshaft.
3. Special valve springs, cups and seats.
4. Two 1¾" S. U. carburetors and necessary attaching parts.
5. A cold-air box for the carburetors.
6. A special advance-curve distributor.
7. A new 4-speed gearbox (overdrive is also standard equipment).

The above items give an engine output of 110 bhp at 4500. Thus the 100M falls between the 90 bhp (at 4000) of the standard 100 model and the 132 bhp at 4700 of the strictly-for-competition 100-S model tested last September. The performance, as might be expected also falls about midway between models, per the following data.

photography
Ralph Poole

Model	100	100M	100S
top speed	102	109	119
0-60 mph	11.7	9.6	7.8
SS ¼ mile	18.1	17.4	16.1

The 100 model was tested in our July, 1954, issue and all data applies to the cars in "showroom" condition; running with top and side curtains installed except on the 100 S which has neither. In addition, the above performance data can be duplicated by the average owner, driving a car in good tune and making brisk but not brutal gear changes. Furthermore, the performance figures given in the tabulation are all the more remarkable when we take note of the fact that this car weighed 235 lbs more than our earlier 100 model test car.

The 100 M has the stiffer Le Mans type rear springs, front shocks and anti-roll bar. Consequently it rides a little firmer than the normal 100 model and in our opinion suffers somewhat in comparison—because of the really excellent ride in the 100. However, there is no denying that the 100 M suspension is better suited for competition work, and the tendency to bottom (at the rear) on fast starts from a standstill is greatly reduced. The test car was also equipped with the latest type Dunlop Road Speed tires which have sipes (small cuts) in the tread. These were a tremendous improvement over earlier equipment, not only on dry roads, but more especially in the wet. Adhesion on slippery curves is almost uncanny.

The new transmission unit is the same as supplied on the 100 S model, but with overdrive added. This is actually a modified Austin "Princess" unit, designed to withstand over 200 ft-lbs of torque. Durability should be almost unlimited.

Our test car was brought over for the Nassau races by Donald Healey, and it garnered a 9th place in class D, beaten by one other A-H and a flock of Ferraris. The driver was Roy Jackson-Moore, who then drove the car to California and was also at the wheel during our performance tests. Despite nearly 5000 miles on the clock, the car was in good condition and got only minor attention (plugs, points and tappets) before the test. Roy reports that at Nassau, with windshield removed, he indicated 4400 rpm on the long straight, equivalent to about 116 mph, with tire expansion. The best we could get during the timed high speed runs was 4150 rpm, due to the extra drag of top and windshield.

As shown in the data panel, the 3rd-od and 4th-direct ratios are nearly identical, consequently all acceleration tests were made by flipping the overdrive switch from direct to od when 4500 rpm was attained in 3rd gear. This gives a quicker shift and better times than using 4th-direct. The engine is red-lined at 4800 rpm, but there was no improvement in acceleration times by exceeding the 4500 rpm point in each gear. The overdrive unit is available with 3 ratio options: .756, .778, or .820. This car was equipped with the .778 ratio which, when multiplied by the rear axle ratio of 4.10, gives an overall ratio of 3.1898. As now supplied, the overdrive is operable at any speed in any gear—in effect 8 speeds forward, 2 in reverse. However, most owners will prefer to use the overdrive only on the open highway as an extra "5th speed" for cruising. Direct drive (4.10) is a very useful gear for city driving, thanks to the very good lugging power of the large, four-cylinder engine. Top speed in direct drive is limited by the red-line—though the engine will run well beyond 5000 rpm in this ratio if allowed to do so.

The "Le Mans" kit is certainly designed to give a worthwhile performance gain, yet still retain the low speed pulling power (torque) and ruggedness of the large, four-cylinder engine. However, the valve timing of the 100 M is still extremely conservative at only 10° overlap, and for those who are not interested in production car competition a reground camshaft can be used to good advantage. Such a change is described this month in "Tune Up Clinic" on page 42.

Other items which are listed by the Austin Company as options include an 18.7 or a 31 gallon fuel tank, Alfin brake drums and aero screens, all at extra cost. A heater is still supplied and included in the price.

The 100 M can be identified at a glance by the hood louvers and leather hood strap. In all other appearance details the car is identical to previous models, though the overdrive switch and the ignition lock have been interchanged. The seats are comfortable, the driving position is just right and there is ample storage space for odds and ends. In fact, the popularity of the Austin-Healey is due to only two things: (1) it's a genuine sports car and (2) it is reliable and trouble free. The 100 M will enhance that reputation.

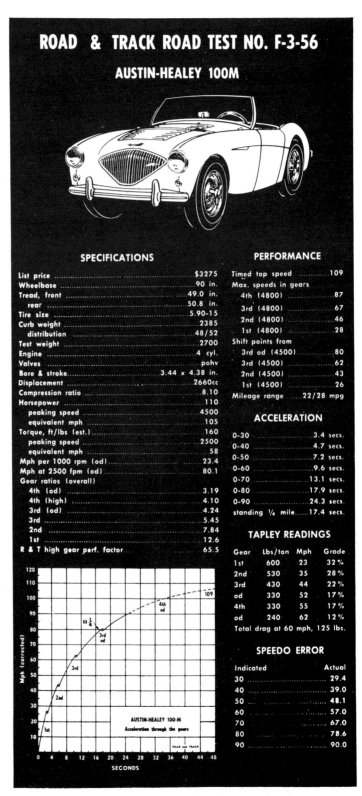

ROAD & TRACK ROAD TEST NO. F-3-56

AUSTIN-HEALEY 100M

SPECIFICATIONS

List price	$3275
Wheelbase	90 in.
Tread, front	49.0 in.
rear	50.8 in.
Tire size	5.90-15
Curb weight	2385
distribution	48/52
Test weight	2700
Engine	4 cyl.
Valves	pohv
Bore & stroke	3.44 x 4.38 in.
Displacement	2660cc
Compression ratio	8.10
Horsepower	110
peaking speed	4500
equivalent mph	105
Torque, ft/lbs (est.)	160
peaking speed	2500
equivalent mph	58
Mph per 1000 rpm (od)	23.4
Mph at 2500 fpm (od)	80.1
Gear ratios (overall)	
4th (od)	3.19
4th (high)	4.10
3rd (od)	4.24
3rd	5.45
2nd	7.84
1st	12.6
R & T high gear perf. factor	65.5

PERFORMANCE

Timed top speed	109
Max. speeds in gears	
4th (4800)	87
3rd (4800)	67
2nd (4800)	46
1st (4800)	28
Shift points from	
3rd od (4500)	80
3rd (4500)	62
2nd (4500)	43
1st (4500)	26
Mileage range	22/28 mpg

ACCELERATION

0-30	3.4 secs.
0-40	4.7 secs.
0-50	7.2 secs.
0-60	9.6 secs.
0-70	13.1 secs.
0-80	17.9 secs.
0-90	24.3 secs.
standing ¼ mile	17.4 secs.

TAPLEY READINGS

Gear	Lbs/ton	Mph	Grade
1st	600	23	32%
2nd	530	35	28%
3rd	430	44	22%
od	330	52	17%
4th	330	55	17%
od	240	62	12%
Total drag at 60 mph, 125 lbs.			

SPEEDO ERROR

Indicated	Actual
30	29.4
40	39.0
50	48.1
60	57.0
70	67.0
80	78.6
90	90.0

AUSTIN-HEALEY 100-M
Acceleration through the gears

ROAD and TRACK

C1

C2

C1. The Grosvenor London Showroom of the Donald Healey Motor Company in 1956 featured this poster which accurately summed up the appeal of the "100".
  Note the breakline in the duo-tone paint at the front wheel arch on this BN2.

C2. As a stylish and attractive car, the "100" was often used for promotional purposes, and is seen here at a 1956 fashion show in a dealer showroom.
  Note that the body side feature line is carried through to the back of the rear wing.

C3. More than thirty years old, this picture shows how boats were often used to provide a background for contemporary advertising material. Taken in 1953, this example is typical of the genre.

C6

C4-C8. From every angle the Austin-Healey 100 has graceful style and immense visual appeal. The integration of its flowing lines and smooth curves shows a degree of perfection seldom achieved in a volume-produced car and quite outstanding at the time of its introduction.

C7

C8

C9

C10

C9. With the windscreen in the lowered position, the car has a beautifully clean profile ...

C10-C12. ... which is obvious from every aspect.

OOM 552

C13

C16

C13. Postwar sports car designs marked the significant change from centrally-hinged bonnet tops and exposed radiators to smooth top panels and concealed radiators. The Healey was one of the first designs to embody this major styling change.

C14. In the early 1950s semaphore turn indicators were still very common and "winker" indicators were somewhat unusual, leading to confusion amongst some drivers! The Healey winking indicators were combined with the side marker lamps; the brake light filament doubling up with that for the winker. By today's standards those indicators are not at all obvious to following drivers who are usually more intent upon trying to read the identity of the car from the boot lid badge! Confusion results!

C15. With hood and side screens raised the car is snug and weatherproof. The large rear window provides good visibility by comparative sports car standards.

C16. Blue trim was one option with white body colour. The transmission tunnel has a padded leather cover.

C14

C15

C17. This view of the cockpit shows the correct silver applique to the instrument binnacle on the fascia, the comfortable well-shaped seats, transmission tunnel-mounted handbrake lever; all to standard specification.

C18. Engine and engine compartment from carburettor side. Polished alloy rocker cover was an optional fitment.

C19. The most popular production colour for the "100" was Carmine Red, followed by Healey Blue and then Old English White. Greens and blacks were produced in somewhat smaller volumes.

C17

C19

C18

C20

C20. The bulk of "100" production was to left-hand-drive specification giving the driver the full benefit of exhaust system heat! (Courtesy Roger Moment, USA).

C21. The front cover and two internal pages from the second edition of the Austin-Healey "100" sales brochure. The prototype car (here re-numbered MWD 360 and taxed for use on the road) was featured on the cover. This car survived in private ownership until the late 1950s but its subsequent fate is unfortunately unknown.

The prototype car was also featured extensively on the inside pages to illustrate the various attributes of the model.

The last page of the catalogue, not shown, contained specifications.

C21

OWNER'S VIEW

In order to gain an insight into those attributes which attract present day owners and enthusiasts to the Austin-Healey 100, I sought the views of two fairly typical owners, one in the UK and one in the United States.

Peter Tanser is a Worcestershire business man with a lifelong enthusiasm for cars, having owned many interesting vehicles ranging from a Dellow trials car to a V-12 E-type Jaguar. His everyday car is a very high performance fuel-injected BMW. Roger Moment is an engineer with an American-owned multi-national company and drives an MGB for daily use. As his wife drives a Volvo and one of his sons owns a Fiat 124 coupé, they are obviously a family oriented towards European cars!

To begin, I asked both men what it was that aroused their interest in the Healey. It was as a Dellow-owning member of the Hagley and District Light Car Club in the mid 1950s that Peter saw his first 100 and knew straight away that he must own one somehow, sometime! The car was beautiful and had an impressive performance which together with its capability of being used in competition by the average clubman gave it an attractive

image. The only barrier to ownership was the price: a thousand pounds was a great deal of money in 1954. Roger's response was very different. In 1967 the movie *The Graduate* was released and featured prominently was Dustin Hoffman's Alfa Romeo Duetto Spyder. This film gave the sports car bug real bite, and many of Roger's friends bought new Fiat 124 Spyders, and Datsun convertibles, but he could not afford such status symbols and had to settle for a 400 dollar well worn 1958 BN6 Austin-Healey. Roger fixed-up this car at a fraction of the cost of a new car and was introduced to the Healey magic.

Seven years later Roger bought his 1955 BN1, having got to know the marque pretty well by then and appreciating the fact that older cars are easier to work on than more modern ones, laden down with emission control devices and the like. He was impressed by the styling and performance, based on his experience with his 100-6. In Peter's case, twenty eight years were to elapse before he bought his ''100''! Passing a local sports car dealer's premises he spotted an Ice Blue over White example and forty eight hours later had clinched a deal and drove the car home. He was not at all disappointed by the experience, but admits it was very different to driving his BMW!

Although Peter's car was in running order, he realised that the overall condition was not too good, a previous owner having cut a section from the rear shroud in an attempt to fix up a child's seat. The overdrive stopped working and the usual fluid leaks began to manifest themselves. Roger's car was a fair condition 50,000 mile, well cared for machine, but had suffered from being used for too many short journeys. Rust damage was apparent in the wings and some suspension wear was evident.

Over the next few years Roger

carried out a mechanical overhaul and then a cosmetic job. Still dissatisfied with the results he eventually embarked on a ground-up restoration and admits that with the benefit of hindsight he would have been better off by being patient and doing the job properly the first time! Shortly after buying his car, Peter, with number two son Julian, went to their first International Healey Day at Weston Park in Shropshire. Having seen some really excellent cars there, they decided that nothing but the best would be good enough for them too, and so began a full scale rebuild of their car, which was to take three and a half years because, very often, business got in the way of pleasure!

Peter feels that if he were ever to rebuild another Healey he would probably buy a car that was as complete as possible but not necessarily a runner as he is sure that one pays dearly to be able to drive the car immediately. He says that to have an enthusiastic son is a great help in undertaking a rebuilding project. Roger endorses the view that it is preferable to buy a complete car, undamaged but worn, and then fix it up yourself. Not only is this the less expensive route, but the owner will know the quality of work going into the job. All too often people buy cars that have received a cosmetic going over only to end up doing much, if not all, the work over again. Knowing the vulnerable points of the car makes it possible to keep a restored Austin-Healey from deteriorating again. Both men saw buying a properly restored Austin-Healey as an alternative, but as such cars are rare and consequently expensive this choice is not really to be recommended.

Spare parts availability was not seen as a major problem, but Peter felt that he was fortunate in buying a car that was virtually complete. Many American suppliers have good stocks, but prices tend to be rather high.

Roger found buying from specialists in England less costly, but had to accept delays of up to two months in receiving the ordered parts. He has used about ten different sources for the parts used in restoring and maintaining his car.

When asked about the performance and handling of their cars, both Peter and Roger said that driving the ''100'' was a lot of fun. Peter thought the car had very good performance and handling for a car of its age, providing that marvellous feeling of driving through the seat of your pants! Roger said that the car was fast, safe at speed and much more responsive than many modern cars. However, because it took so much time and effort to restore, it does not now get driven as frequently as when first owned. This tends to be the case with Peter's car too, but he considers it to be as practical as any sports car of its type. He did not consider running costs to be high and neither did Roger who finds his car returns around 25mpg with the limited running involved.

Both cars have been prize winners in Concours events but in view of their high presentational qualities, neither has been entered in competitive driving events. Neither owner wants to expose cherished cars to the risk of accidental damage, and Roger made the important point that it is hardly fair to subject a thirty years old car to competitive stresses. If a vital component should fail, the consequences could be serious.

Flourishing owners' clubs in the UK and across the United States have been of great help to Peter and Roger. Both said that the clubs had provided technical help and introduced them to a wide circle of like-minded enthusiasts, some of whom had become good friends. Roger was really in the dark on a number of details of the 100 which were eventually clarified by Club members. He has come to the conclusion that the more he learns the more he still has to learn: a view shared by this writer. One has to be very careful about being too assertive about points of detail, because there is always an unexpected contradiction lurking around the next corner!

A-H Spares was named as having been particularly helpful to Peter, Roger agreed but said he had also found Southern Carburetters very helpful: both businesses holding comprehensive stocks. Roger found the mail order services offered by such companies vital to him in his rebuild programme.

Both agreed that much of their enjoyment of ownership came from the work of restoration and seeing the results at the end of their projects. It seems that the anticipation of finishing the rebuild gives as much pleasure as its actual achievement! The wide spread of friendships arising from ownership was also much appreciated.

In conclusion Peter and Roger were asked what advice they would give to potential owners of an Austin-Healey 100. Peter made the point that even after a comprehensive rebuild, an owner must be prepared to give a thirty year old car a great deal of continuous love and care, a view shared by Roger who also felt that it was necessary to get to know problem areas and how to cope with them. Such knowledge will be invaluable in judging what is a fair asking price for a particular car.

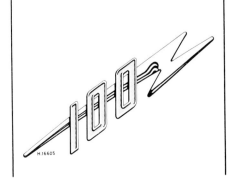

H.16605

BUYING

When it is realised that the youngest Austin-Healey 100 is now very nearly thirty years old it will be appreciated that the possibility of finding an example in good original condition is extremely remote although very occasionally an exceptionally good car does come to the market. Consequently the aspiring owner is faced with the choice of buying either a neglected and maybe incomplete car, an apparently clean and tidy car, or a fully restored example. Since the BN1 model constituted the major part of production, these are the cars which appear most frequently for sale, with the BN2 being comparatively rare. The factory Le Mans derivative of the BN2 is very rare indeed and would command a premium price whatever its condition. After-market conversions to 100M specification can also be found, but care should be taken to ensure that the description is in fact accurate because quite often the fitting of only a louvred bonnet or the larger H6 carburetters has been used to attribute the ''M'' designation to an otherwise standard specification car.

Fifteen to twenty years ago, the Austin-Healey was just another ageing sports car wich could be outperformed by the then new generation of small sporting saloons and consequently it became almost worthless. As a result, many vehicles found their way into the hands of poseurs who butchered and modified them to an alarming extent without regard for the originality and character of the car. At the same time many cars were scrapped for reasons which today would seem unjustified. These actions reduced the number of cars remaining to the point where prices inevitably began to rise again, and this is a trend which can only continue as the number of cars available is limited and demand increasing.

The worth of a car is the price the vendor expects to obtain for it on the one hand and the price a purchaser is willing to pay for it on the other hand, so that it is impossible to quote specific price guidelines. Many vendors seem to take the view that even a derelict hulk is worth a substantial sum, based on the belief that after an easy restoration job the car will have a high value and that they have an entitlement to benefit from this enhancement before it is achieved! Restoration is neither cheap nor easy, and potential owners should be quite clear in their own minds what they expect of their cars before commiting themselves to what could turn into an expensive and demoralising adventure.

Frequently offered for sale are cars upon which much time and money have been expended, both having become exhausted before the project is completed. The vendor will invariably pitch the asking price to recover all outstanding costs in the belief that this is reasonable and justifiable, which it is not, since the calibre of work carried out may not be to an adequate standard for the purchaser. Most prospective purchasers cherish the idea of owning a 100 points condition car without appreciating the very high costs involved in achieving this objective and failing to realise that total restoration costs to reach this standard can exceed the market value of the finished vehicle.

For the enthusiast who is determined to own a first class car, the choice lies between buying a car which has been fully restored to known and approved standards by a recognised restoration expert specialising in the marque, or buying a vehicle in need of total restoration and then spending a great deal of money with the same specialists. Alternatively, if possessed of adequate skill and determination, owners can do much of the work themselves to hold costs down, but some tasks will almost certainly need to be carried out by specialists. If the restoration route is chosen, then the buyer should pay the lowest possible price for the base vehicle. This may appear to be stating the obvious, but there is no point in spending a large sum on what amounts to a licence to spend a great deal more money. Several cars should be looked at before making a choice and hasty decisions should be resisted because ill considered actions can often result in much distress at a later date when the magnitude of the task ahead is revealed.

Equally, there is no point in paying quite a large sum for what appears to be an 80 points car in the belief that a modest outlay will bring it up to 100 point standard. The new owner will almost certainly end up totally rebuilding the car as various shortcomings are exposed, at an enormous total cost which would bear no relation to the value of the completed vehicle. This reinforces the caveat that prospective owners should be clear as to what they expect of their cars. Do they want to participate in Concours d'Elegance competitions, or will they be satisfied with a good reliable car which can be enjoyed at a practical level, without worrying about small details of specification and perfection of presentation?

Reconciling their requirements with their means and capabilities will avoid much anguish at a later stage. In any event it should be understood that the purchase and restoration of an Austin-Healey 100 to top class condition is not a venture to be undertaken by the financially faint hearted, but because values of high quality cars will be maintained as the demand for those remaining examples is sustained, the investment can be considered to be sound.

If there are no financial constraints and the buyer chooses to purchase a top class car, then it is really only necessary to check where the work was done, to be reasonably satisfied as to the quality of the vehicle, although it is always a wise safeguard to seek the views of an independent expert because sometimes as a matter of either expediency or necessity, some deviation from original specification may have been introduced.

If seeking a car for restoration there are many problem areas to check out, some safety-critical and some specification-related. Because of the age of the cars, many will have been modified or "improved" by the replacement of correct specification parts with non-original items when either wear or damage had their effects on the original part. A fairly common example of this problem is the horn push and trafficator control switch assembly. This is frequently missing and is virtually impossible to obtain, so its absence, and the absence of similar detail parts, should certainly be used as a bargaining counter.

When the Austin-Healey was designed, the effects of mud traps built in were not appreciated and the whole car is extremely vulnerable to rust attack. In particular, the outer body skin panels are certain to have been affected and in some cases may have been replaced by glass fibre replica parts. These will certainly diminish the value of a car. Where

the original steel wing panels remain on the car they will be rust damaged along their lower edges and at the return flanges at the front and rear door pillars, which themselves will also be severely attacked. Sill sections at the point where the wings attach, and below the doors, will also be affected with rust damage, possibly extending into the floor panels. Replacement steel panels for all affected areas are now available from specialist suppliers, but in some cases it will be preferable to repair front wings in order to preserve both a good fit and the correct front wheel opening which is critical to appearance.

Front and rear body centre section shroud panels are pressed from aluminium and with age tend to develop cracks at the corner radii of bonnet and boot openings. They are also liable to suffer electrolytic corrosion along the edge flanges where the steel outer wing panels bolt up to them. Although these problems can be rectified by a skilled body repair man, particular attention should be paid to the examination of the shroud panels to check for accident damage which can be very difficult to repair and reshape to a satisfactory standard. Replacement shrouds are not available so condition of these parts is a critical factor in the choice of a car.

Although of robust design the chassis frame is susceptible to rust attack and accident damage. The side members should be straight

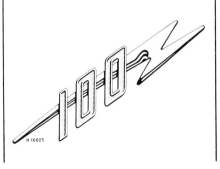

H.16605

and parallel from front to rear with no evidence of bending as the result of a front end collision. Front corner impacts will usually push the top suspension mounting backwards and the lower rear wishbone arm inwards to produce a nasty dog-leg bend in the chassis side members, extending as far back as the toe box floor panel. A severe kerb strike on a front wheel can produce similar chassis damage to a lesser degree.

Because the front damper attachment screws tend to work loose the captive nuts in the mounting platform are liable to fretting and eventual stripping and in extreme cases the plate itself can tear out. Fortunately, repair plates are now available to solve what was a difficult repair problem. Invariably the bottom face of the front crossmember will be damaged where thoughtless owners have jacked up the very heavy front end of the car without placing a bearer between the jack pad and the member. Sometimes the damage, combined with rusting, can be so severe as to leave large holes in this area.

Chassis side outriggers supporting the floor and sill panels are also liable to rusting, especially at the rear where there is less protection by oil film blown back from the engine bay. Of particular importance in this area are the rear spring shackle mountings on the rear outriggers, since these can tear away under load if rusting is severe. The rear crossmember is particularly vulnerable to rust and damage, as unlike the front crossmember it receives no protection from oil film but is still used as a jacking point. In this same general area, the rear shackle pins are liable to seizure in their bushes unless regular routine greasing has been carried out and this is a task which is most unlikely to have been attended to on a car which has had many owners.

Also at the back end of the chassis, the rear damper mounting plates can tend to cause cracks to develop in the sides of the members due to the longitudinal twisting stresses set up in them by the resistive action of the dampers. Simple welding can effect a cure to this problem. Fortunately, repair sections covering all problem areas are available from the specialist suppliers so that the essential structural integrity of the chassis may be restored.

Provided the seats are reasonably intact, the interior should present few problems, as reproduction materials are freely available to permit a first class re-trimming job to be carried out by the competent owner. Seats can, however, present a problem, especially if the car has been badly neglected. If the frames remain then the seats can be rebuilt, but this work is best carried out by a skilled coach trimmer if a good result is to be obtained, and this is essential as the seats can make or mar the appearance of the interior of the car. In some cases the seats will have been replaced by non-original design parts and this can present a serious problem because, apart from ready made re-trimming kits, the basic seats are not available except as second hand parts from someone who has broken up a car. They can be difficult to find.

Major mechanical assemblies, with the exception of early BN1 gearboxes, are generally robust, reliable and easily rebuilt. The BN1 gearbox that is derived from the A79/A90 unit is the Achilles heel of early models, being extremely prone to failure of what are the third speed gear pairs in the box, but which fulfil the function of second speed gear in the Austin-Healey application. From gearbox number 5146, gears with improved tooth forms were introduced which largely overcame the problem. Later gear sets are not interchangeable with earlier ones so that in cases of gearbox failure, either the complete set of internals must be changed for the

later design or a replacement gearbox found. New gearbox internals are not available, but certain specialists can provide reconstructed gears if the better alternative of a replacement gearbox cannot be followed. The BN2 car uses the later design BMC "C" Series conventional four-speed gearbox which is both strong and durable. All cars featured Laycock overdrive as standard and these are usually very reliable unless allowed to run with insufficient oil. Rebuilding of these units by specialists is straightforward.

Rear axles are strong and generally trouble free, but the splined hub extensions should be checked for corrosion and fretting wear resulting from inadequate greasing and running with improperly tightened knock-off nuts. Wheels will invariably have broken and loose spokes and may have worn internal hub splines for the same reasons that the hub extensions will be showing signs of damage. Wheels are most easily dealt with by straight exchange from specialist suppliers.

On a car which has covered many thousands of miles in the hands of several owners who may have been less than prudent in carrying out essential routine maintenance tasks, the front suspension will undoubtedly be showing signs of serious wear, especially at the lower wishbone arm outer end fulcrum pins. It is essential to the inherently good handling characteristics of the car that the front suspension and steering system is in first class order. The difference in feel between a "loose" car and one that has properly set up suspension is quite dramatic. Great care and attention should be paid to ensuring that all suspension and brake system parts are renewed and brought up to new car condition in view of the high performance potential of the car. The need to have a thirty year old, obviously fast and attractive car in

first class mechanical condition cannot be over emphasised if the hostility of the authorities is not to be aroused in the unfortunate event of some mishap occurring on the road. Since all parts to achieve a well set-up car are readily available from many sources there is no excuse for not having the car in a safe and roadworthy condition.

The big four-cylinder engine is a heavy and lightly stressed unit but prone to oil leaks from crankshaft seals at both ends. There is little that can be done about the rear end leak which is due to the design of the now old-fashioned scroll seal used. This works well when the shaft is revolving but is ineffective when the engine is stationary. Do not be surprised to find copious quantities of oil all over the whole power unit. This is not serious and is merely symptomatic of an old design. There is a universal and persistent seepage of coolant along the cylinder head joint on the spark plug side. This is due to capillary action by the asbestos interlayer in the head gasket which cannot be completely eliminated, but can be minimised to an acceptable degree at the rebuilding stage by having both joint faces machined flat and pulling the cylinder head nuts down to 85 lb/ft torque with an accurately calibrated wrench. Poor coolant circulation at the rear of the block can cause sludging to develop in the internal passages sufficient in some cases to force out the welch plug in the rear face. As there is only a small clearance here between the engine and the fire wall, this can be very difficult to replace with the engine *in situ*. Air cleaners have often been removed by amateur tuners and until recently were very difficult to find. Acceptable replica parts are now available to preserve correct underbonnet appearance.

The electrical system is straightforward but may require rewiring in parts as the original cotton braiding on the harness may have rotted away and the bullet connectors may have been attacked by corrosion. First class reproduction harnesses are now available to remedy these problems. However, authentic 6 volt batteries used in pairs are no longer available so that in many cases a conversion to a single 12 volt battery will have been made. Usually these single batteries have been quite large which has meant putting them in the boot and making untidy connections to the existing main leads. Today, a better solution is to use one of the new smaller 12 volt batteries which will locate in the same place as one of the original 6 volt units. This will preserve the interior boot appearance and remain close to original specification. Alternatively, original batteries can be replated

by some specialists, but the cost far exceeds the cost of a new single 12 volt battery. Choice will be governed by the extent to which an owner wishes to preserve original specification details.

By now it will be realised that rebuilding to whatever standard is desired is entirely feasible, restricted only by the resources and degree of commitment of the owner. If possible the chosen car should be a BN2 since this model overcomes the shortcomings of the BN1 which nevertheless remains

an enjoyable car. In general, choose a car from one end or the other of the whole price spectrum of cars available. Buy carefully, spend wisely and enjoy one of the all time great British sports cars from an era never to return.

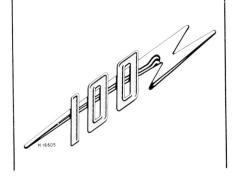

H.16605

CLUBS, SPECIALISTS & BOOKS

Clubs

In common with other classic car marques there is a flourishing worldwide network of Clubs operating for the benefit of owners of all Austin-Healey cars. Since the largest single market for the Austin-Healey was the United States of America, it is not surprising that there are most clubs in that country. Because of the enormous geographical spread of the US it is impracticable for there to be one central focus so individual clubs have been set up to serve the needs of specific areas, although there are now the first signs of a move towards federation with a view to co-ordinating activities and resources. Much the same problem arises in Australia, again because of the sheer size of the country, with clubs serving major areas of population.

In the UK the Austin-Healey Club Ltd is the co-ordinating body for seven autonomous club centres, serving the needs of the country on a regional basis.

There are also Clubs in the Continental European and Scandinavian countries, in South Africa and in New Zealand, so that in almost all territories where the cars were sold, the owner has the opportunity of enjoying the undoubted benefits which arise from membership of a club devoted to the preservation and enjoyment of the Austin-Healey in all its variations.

Although membership of an Austin-Healey Club is not an essential concomitant of ownership of an Austin-Healey car, there is much to be gained from joining the appropriate area group since this brings one into contact with like-minded enthusiasts with a substantial reservoir of know-how about the cars, or those parts, sometimes difficult to find, required to complete a restoration project. There can be social benefits and the worthwhile introductions to specialist insurance brokers who can arrange cover on more favourable terms than are available on the open market. There will be local area meetings and, usually, an annual large-scale gathering involving several centres or areas. In the UK this event is International Healey Weekend; on the Eastern side of the USA the annual "Encounter" is held whilst the Central States of the continent organize "Conclave". To attend any of these big meetings is an occasion of sublime pleasure for the Austin-Healey enthusiast.

Britain

Mrs Carol Marks
Austin-Healey Club
171 Coldharbour Road
Bristol BS6 7SX
England.

Australia

Austin-Healey Owners Club
94 Links Avenue
Concord 2137
New South Wales.

The Austin-Healey Club of
Western Australia
P.O. Box 70
Maylands 6051
Western Australia.

Austin-Healey Owners Club South
Australia
P.O. Box 10
Norwood 5067
South Australia

Austin-Healey Owners Club
Queensland
P.O. Box Broadway
Brisbane 4000
Queensland
Australia.

Austin-Healey Owners Club
Victoria
P.O. Box 105 Kew
Victoria 3101
Australia.

Austin-Healey Owners Club
(N.S.W.)
P.O. Box A471
Sydney South 2001
Australia.

Austria

Austin-Healey Club Austria
A1220 Wien
Plankenmaistrasse 20
Austria.

Belgium

Austin-Healey Club Belgie
Kappiteldreef 70
9831 St. Martins Latum
Belgium.

Canada

Canadian Austin-Healey Club
Ottawa Centre
P.O. Box 2025, Station D
Ottawa
Ontario
Canada.

Austin-Healey Association British
Columbia
P.O. Box 80274
Burnaby
British Columbia V5H 3X5
Canada.

Denmark

Austin-Healey Club Denmark
Viekaer 22
2950 Vedbaek
Denmark.

France

Austin-Healey Club France
35 Quai de Grenelle
Paris 75015
France.

Germany

Austin-Healey Club Germany
Leopoldstrasse 24a
D7500 Karlsruhe 1
Germany.

Holland

Austin-Healey Owners Club
Netherlands
P. Bernhardlaan 15
2741 DV Waddinxveen
Holland.

Japan

Austin-Healey Club Japan
c/o Masahiro Ishikawa
26 – 3 Shibimata 5 – Chome
Katsushika – Ku
Tokyo
Japan.

New Zealand

Austin-Healey Car Club New
Zealand
P.O. Box 25 – 016
St. Heliers
Auckland
New Zealand.

Austin-Healey Club New Zealand
143 Oraria Road
Johnsville
Wellington
New Zealand.

South Africa

Austin-Healey Club South Africa
P.O. Box 33342
Jeppestown
South Africa.

Sweden

Austin-Healey Club Sweden
Albatrossvagen 86
S136 66 Handen
Sweden.

Switzerland

Austin-Healey Club Switzerland
Uberland Strasse 199A
CH 8600 Dubendorf
Switzerland.

United States of America

Austin-Healey Club Pacific Centre
P.O. Box 6197
San José
California 95150
U.S.A.

Austin-Healey Club of America
603 E. Euclid
Arlington Heights
Illinois 60004
U.S.A.

Florida Association of
Austin-Healey Clubs
12408 N.56 Street
Tampa
Florida
U.S.A.

North Texas Austin-Healey Club
P.O. Box 45332
Dallas
Texas 75245
U.S.A.

Austin-Healey Club Oregon
P.O. Box 4532
Portland
Oregon 97208
U.S.A.

Austin-Healey Club San Diego
P.O. Box 2367
San Diego
California 92112
U.S.A.

Austin-Healey Association of
Southern California
P.O. Box 4082
Riverside
California 92514
U.S.A.

Austin-Healey Sports and Touring
Club
P.O. Box 360
N. Baldwin
New York 11510
U.S.A.

Specialists

Following the end of production of the "Big Healey" in the late 1960s, the recognised source of spare parts for the Austin-Healey 100 was the Donald Healey Motor Company and those original BMC franchise holders which had stocks remaining. In 1970 the Healey Motor Co. discontinued the supply of parts for these cars and agreed to their Parts Manager, Mr. Fred Draper, buying out their remaining stock and establishing A-H Spares Ltd, which has become perhaps the best known and certainly the oldest specialist supplier of Austin-Healey parts. In 1974, enthusiasts David Jeffrey and Laurence Mahon founded Southern Carburettors which has now grown to be the largest manufacturer of Big Healey spares in the world. Between them, these two companies dominate the spare parts market in the UK and supply agencies and individuals worldwide with a justified excellent reputation for quality and prompt service. In the United States the best known supplier is perhaps Moss Motors Ltd, who also handle parts for other BMC classic cars.

As interest in the marque has increased in recent years, a number of specialist restoration shops have opened up, some good and some bad, to handle the requirements of those owners who, for whatever reason, prefer to have their cars rebuilt by professionals. It is quite impossible to comment upon the merits of these establishments except to say that reputations become known by word of mouth through the clubs, and owners should satisfy themselves as to the competence of a business by personal inspection before placing work in its hands. Owners needing professional help in rebuilding or repairing their cars may consider approaching any of the businesses in the following, by no means exhaustive, list of service companies. Inclusion in this list should not be taken to imply any recommendation and exclusion should not be regarded as criticism. It is simply not possible to be aware of all the diverse businesses operating in this field.

Specialist Parts Suppliers.

A-H Spares Ltd
Unit 7, Westfield Road
Southam Industrial Estate
Southam
Warwickshire CV33 0JH
England.

Telephone: 0926–817181 (Spare parts of every description. Friendly, courteous
and expert service).

Southern Carburettors
Unit 14
Oakwood Industrial Park
Gatwick Road
Crawley
Sussex RH10 2AZ
England.
Telephone: 0293–547841 (Full spare parts service. Comprehensive and efficient
Catalogue available).

Burlen Services
Greencroft Street
Salisbury
Wiltshire SP1 1JF
England.
Telephone 07222–21777
(Carburetter Specialists)

M.C. Griffiths (Auto Components) Ltd
13 Prince Close
North Way
Walworth Industrial Estate
Andover
Hants, SP10 5LD,
England
Telephone: 0264–3650.

The Vintage and Classic Spares Company
Unit 43B Hartlebury Trading Estate
Near Kidderminster
Worcestershire DY10 4JB
England.
Telephone 0299–251353 (An Aladdin's cave of Lucas electrical components, and light units. Prompt worldwide mail-order service).

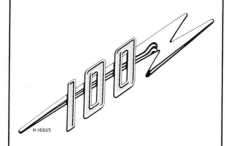

Moss Motors Ltd
P.O. Box MG
Goleta
California 93116
United States of America.
Telephone: 800–235–6954 (except California)
800–322–6985 (California).
(Comprehensive catalogue [AHY–03] available at a cost of 3 dollars)

Scarborough Faire Inc
1151 Main Street
Pawtucket
Rhode Island 02860
United States of America.
Telephone: 401–724–4200.

Hemphill's Healey Haven
4–B Winters Lane
Baltimore
Maryland 21228
U.S.A.
Telephone: 301–788–2291

A.W. Bell Nominees Pty Ltd
4–6 King Street
Oakleigh 3166
Victoria
Australia.
Telephone: 03–568–4622.

Restoration and repair services.

Generally, the following businesses' principal activities are restoration and repair, but in some cases a spare parts service is also available.

K and J B Restorations Ltd
The Croft
Back Lane
Long Lawford
Warwickshire
England.
Telephone 0788–78848 (The establishment of the expert Keith Boyer. Very competent and detailed service covering all aspects from full restoration to minor repairs).

Ellis and Son Restorations
Rothersthorpe Crescent
Northampton NN4 9JD
England.
Telephone: 0604–61487.
(Although Peter Ellis and his son specialise in bodywork, they can also offer a full restoration service when required. Friendly and efficient service).

JME
4A Wise Terrace
Leamington Spa
Warwickshire
England.
Telephone: 0962–640031 (Full restoration service).

Hardy Engineering
268 Kingston Road
Leatherhead
Surrey
England.
Telephone: 0372–378927
(Gearbox and rear axle specialists. Comprehensive range of units held in stock. Work also carried out on customers' own units).

Healey Surgeons Inc
7211 Carroll Avenue
Takoma Park
Maryland 20912
U.S.A.
Telephone: 301–270-8811.
(Complete restoration service backed up by comprehensive parts catalogue. Proprietors – Bruce and Inan Phillips).

British Car Center
Norman Nock Imported Cars Inc
2060 N Wilson Way
Stockton, CA 95205.
U.S.A.
Telephone: 948–8767 for service and 462–6016 for parts. (Expert service and restoration business run by Lucas factory-trained UK expatriate Norman Nock and family).

Walsh Motor Works
651 E. Argues Avenue
Sunnyvale
California 94086
United States of America.
Telephone: 408–245-8502
(Restoration and repair service backed by 20 years' experience).

Sports Cars Restored
Walter Blanck
705 Dimmeydale Deerfield
Illinois 60015
U.S.A.
Telephone: 312/945–1360
(Consultant and parts service by mail-order).

Books

It was not until seven years after the introduction of the Austin-Healey 100 that the first book on the marque appeared in 1960. This was *The Austin-Healey* ghosted for Donald Healey and Tommy Wisdom; it covered all the then–existing models up to the 3000 Mk1 and the Mark 1 Sprite. Also in 1960, Pearsons published *Austin-Healey Cars* by C.P. Davidson, which is a useful and concise guide to the service and maintenance of the same models.

Ten years later, in June 1970, came *Healeys and Austin-Healeys* by Peter Browning and Les Needham, past secretaries of the Austin-Healey Club when this was backed by BMC. This book was last published by Haynes/Foulis but is currently out of print.

Then in the late 1970s with the rising interest in the marque, came Geoffrey Healey's definitive history of the cars entitled *Austin-Healey, the Story of the Big Healeys,* followed three years later by his second volume of interest to "Big Healey" enthusiasts, *Healey, the Specials.* These two books,

published by Haynes/Gentry, are essential reading for all Austin-Healey *aficionados* and tell the inside story of the conception and development of the cars.

In 1978 the prolific writer Chris Harvey produced his copiously illustrated *Healey the Handsome Brute.* Published by Haynes/Oxford Illustrated Press.

In 1981, Classic Car expert Graham Robson added *The Big Healeys* to MRP's Collectors Guide Series, a very comprehensive study of all the Big Healeys.

From Motorbooks International in the United States in 1984 came the *Illustrated Austin-Healey Buyers Guide* by Richard Newton. Obviously directed mainly at the US enthusiast, this book provides entertaining reading and covers all models, but with the emphasis on the big cars.

Brooklands Books and *Road & Track* provide compilations of reprints of contemporary road tests and new car descriptions. There are also two "Year Books" covering the years 1978 and 1979/80 containing informative chapters on the history of the cars, compiled by Paul Skilleter.

Of interest to all Austin-Healey owners will be *The Seven Year Twitch* by former BMC Competitions Manager Marcus Chambers; *Sleepless Knights* by John Sprinzel, and *More Healeys* by Geoffrey Healey.

Although some of the earlier publications have been out of print for many years, careful searching at autojumbles can often be rewarding in building up a personal library of Austin-Healey books.

PHOTO GALLERY

1

1. Controls and instruments are neatly grouped in front of the driver. The 16$\frac{1}{2}$ inch diameter thin-rimmed steering wheel, with central horn and direction indicator switch, fronts a symmetrically arranged instrument layout. Switches, to fall close to hand, are located close to the steering wheel rim.

2. 6000rpm tachometer is 'red-lined' at 4800rpm: quite fast enough for a big and heavy 4-cylinder engine!

3. Speedometer reads to 120mph, some 15mph in excess of the maximum speed potential of the car in standard tune.

2

3

4

5

4. Early production cars carried the classic "Austin-of-England" badge on the boot lid. In the summer of 1954 this was superseded by ...

5. ... "Austin Healey" which ran through to the end of 'Big' Healey production. This change was coincident with the introduction of the rear reflectors.

6. The boot lid lock uses the same key as ignition switch to provide security for the petrol tank filler cap.

7. The spare wheel is secured by a tie bar and strap. These two items are fairly rare, frequently having been discarded in the past by careless owners.

8. Short neck filler tube and cap are concealed within the luggage compartment. The tank top forms the boot floor, which has an "Armacord" covering.

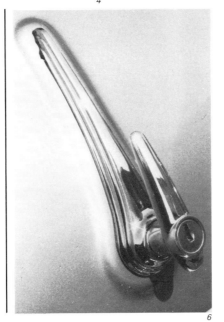

6

7

8

9. Luggage space is particularly generous, especially when compared with other contemporary cars and is quite adequate for the requirements of two people.

10. Overdrive engagement is electrically controlled from a fascia-mounted toggle switch. This is the BN1 switch. That for the BN2 has a circular escutcheon plate and is mounted where the BN1 ignition switch is located. BN2 ignition switch is fitted in the centre of the fascia in the position previously occupied by the BN1 overdrive switch.

11. Polished cast aluminium cylinder head covers are an easily fitted "dress-up" accessory to enhance engine compartment appearance.

12. Austin-Healey wing badge is developed from the original Healey cars and badge and carried through on all subsequent 'Big' Healeys.

13. The distinctive radiator grille was derived from the original Westland and Elliott Healey grille. The smooth curve of the top run was a modification from the peaked form on the prototype car. Grille bars are in satin chrome finish with a bright chrome surround.

9

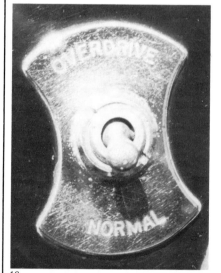

10

11

12

13

14.

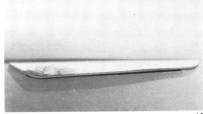

15

16

17

18

14. Normal headlamp specification was a 36 watt unit with block pattern lens, but the shielded bulb type shown here was a popular aftermarket substitution, being more powerful and attractive looking. Correctly, the side marker lights should have the pearl finish to the inside of the lens as seen here.

15. The side flash conceals a ventilation opening in the front wing and spearheads body side feature line.

16. Alfin brake drums were a costly option (£8 each in 1954) listed in the "Le Mans Tuning Booklet" for the BN1. This is the later design, the earlier type having circumferential ribs.

17. Early production cars were fitted with a spiral bevel rear axle with 11 inch diameter x 1³/4 inch wide brake drums. This axle is easily identified by the four stud fixing for the splined wheel hub extension.

18. Later production BN1 cars and all BN2 cars were fitted with a very strong, but heavier, hypoid bevel rear axle. This axle is characterised by the wider brake drum, increased to 2¹/4 inches, and the five stud fixing for the splind hub extension.

19. All Austin-Healey 100 cars were built with 48 spoke wire wheels, shod with 5.90 x 15 Dunlop Road Speed tyres of crossply construction. When compared with modern, low aspect ratio ply tyres, the Michelin crossply tyre seen here appears very large in diameter and narrow in the tread. Clearance to the wheel opening is minimal and was increased by $1^3/_4$ inches for BN2 cars.

20. The smooth flanks and beautiful contours of the bodyshell are well illustrated in this attractive view of the car. A full length tonneau cover was supplied as standard with all new cars.

21. Second series side screen with hand-signalling flap introduced at the end of December 1953. These flaps were also a US market requirement to permit easy payment of turnpike toll charges.

22. The Austin-Healey 100 is one of the very few sports cars which still looks attractive with the hood erected. Much care was taken to ensure a good appearance for the hood.

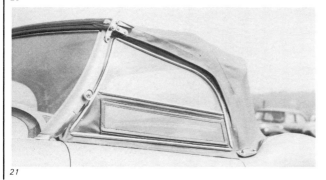

23.

24.

25.

23. Well shaped and comfortable bucket seats for driver and passenger are expensively upholstered with Connolly leather to the wearing surfaces.

24. In contrast with many sports cars of the time, the cockpit is very spacious and comfortable, with the fascia panel being swept upwards over the passenger's side to increase the impression of space.

25. Conversion of the steering column control A70 gearbox to a floorshift necessitated the use of a long lever emerging from the side of the transmission tunnel. Left-hand-drive cars had a much shorter and neater lever.

26. For the 1956 model year, significant changes were introduced with the BN2 model. Ignition and overdrive switches were relocated and a 4-speed gearbox with conventional shift pattern was fitted. The transmission tunnel cover was redesigned to suit the new box. (Courtesy "The Motor").

26.

27

27. The distinctive Healey flash with "100" type designation superimposed, is a feature carried on the radiator grille of all 'Big' Healeys to the 3000 MkI.

28. A unique feature of the 100 is the arrangement for folding down the windscreen. Pins in the bottom of the screen frame relocate into feet fixed into the wing to shroud joint, and swinging links pivoting from the screen stanchions support the assembly clear of the bodywork.

29. Security springs tension the assembly in the folded position. In order to ensure accurate fitting of the screen assembly to the body and to avoid stressing and cracking of the glass, the support stanchions were individually fitted and given idetification numbers.

30. 9 inch Trico "Rainbow" windscreen wiper blades park on the right-hand side of the screen. Curved windscreen glass was a styling advance over other contemporary sports cars which were all limited to flat glass screens.

31. A pull-up handbrake is located on the right-hand side of the driveshaft tunnel. Careful adjustment is necessary to avoid excessive travel and to keep MoT examiners happy!

28

29

30

31

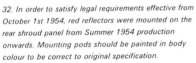

32

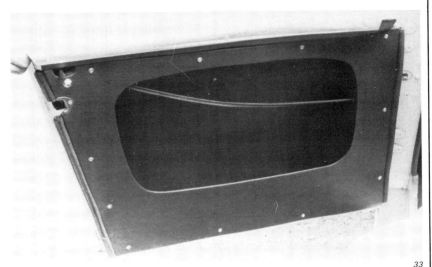

33

32. In order to satisfy legal requirements effective from October 1st 1954, red reflectors were mounted on the rear shroud panel from Summer 1954 production onwards. Mounting pods should be painted in body colour to be correct to original specification.

33. Spacious door pockets add to the substantial carrying capacity of the roomy cockpit. Door catch release is by pull cord within the aperture.

34. When lowered, the hood is concealed behind the seats. Raising can be achieved by a single person, but the task is more easily accomplished by two people working together.

35. Snap action toggle fasteners secure the front hood rail to the top of the windscreen. Fixing is quick and effective with a good seal along the screen edge.

36. The BMC "C" Series 4-speed gearbox fitted to the BN2 had a cast iron case and overcame many of the shortcomings of the BN1 3-speed unit. However, it was still penalised by the offset shift lever resulting from conversion from a saloon car application with steering column change. (Courtesy "The Motor").

34

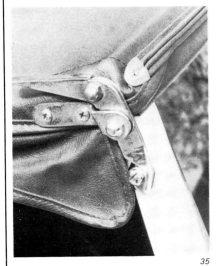

35

36

38

39

40

37. A sentiment which today's owners will confirm is as valid as it was thirty years ago, when this advertisement appeared in motoring magazines!

38. A very special derivative of the normal production Austin Healey 100 was the 100S. The limited production run of 50 cars were all built at Warwick, with all-aluminium bodies and disc brakes all round.

39. The BMC Holland Park showroom featured a special display in August 1953 of the Austin-Healey 100, following its successful launch in the United States.

40. Factory converted BN2 100M photographed at Guy's Cliff, Warwick, in March 1956. Note that the cockpit trim rails are covered in leathercloth to match interior trim. Windscreen washers and racing tyres are fitted and, contrary to popular myth, the grille badge does not have an "M" addition.

41. Left-hand side view of engine compartment. The chromium plated rocker cover was available from Warwick on an exchange basis as a set with the air cleaners. In this example, the standard crackle black finish to the air cleaner is retained. (Courtesy Paul Skilleter).

42. Donald Healey and Sir Leonard Lord pose outside the Longbridge Administration Building prior to the US promotional tour.

43. The prototype car photographed at Longbridge. Note the low headlamp height and distinctive peak to the radiator grille. It appears that the car is still fitted with the 10 inch diameter brakes as originally built with disc wheels.

44. This photograph of the manifold's side of the engine has been carefully airbrushed by the artist for reproduction in advertising literature in the typical style of the 1950s and early '60s.

41

42

43

44

45. By November 1953, production at Longbridge had built up to programme, and the cars were coming off the line at an average rate of 100 per week. Sharp-eyed readers will note that the car at the extreme left of this photograph is about to have the bonnet lid repainted. The "100" was very carefully built and finished.

46. 1955 photograph of a BN1 fitted with the Universal Laminations-manufactured hardtop available from Warwick. The sliding window side screens were specific to this accessory and were not a standard production line fitment.

47. Contemporary BMC publicity photograph taken at Barnt Green Reservoir in the late summer of 1955.

48. Pre-production BN1 engine photographed in March 1953. Tests of development cars quickly indicated the need for a four blade fan to achieve satisfactory cooling on volume production cars, especially when oprating in certain US markets.

49. Third series side screen introduced in February 1955 featured an improved full-length-opening signalling flap.

45

46

47

48

49

50

51

52

50. An October 1953 photograph at Longbridge showing the elegant one-piece 5mm thick Perspex, original specification side screens. Note the damage to the boot lid!

51. Side screens with hand-signalling flaps had a small security strap with "Lift-Dot" fastener to the inside door trim panel. (Courtesy Roger Moment, USA).

52. From chassis 219000 onwards, the engine number became coincident with that for the chassis with either a 1B or BN1 or BN2 prefix as appropriate. In fact, chassis 219000 was allocated to an A70 car, and the first Healey to carry the new combined car/engine number was 219001, built 31st August 1954. Earlier cars carried their chassis plate on the top of the right-hand chassis rail near to the brake master cylinder mounting bracket. All cars carried their body number

plate in the location shown here. (Courtesy Roger Moment, USA).

53. An advanced styling feature of the "100" was the 'tumblehome' of the body side panels. Curved panels of this type were beyond the capabilities of other volume manufacturers in 1952 but are widely used on 1980 cars.

54. The Austin-Healey 100 was supplied with a very comprehensive tool kit, enabling the owners to handle most routine maintenance and repair tasks. (Courtesy Roger Moment, USA).

55. Right-hand side of engine showing correct spark plug lead connectors. On this left-hand-drive car, the brake fluid reservoir can be seen in the top left-hand corner. (Courtesy Roger Moment, USA).

53

54

55

56

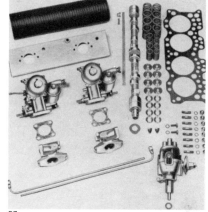

57

58

59

60

56. Although listed as an accessory in the Special Tuning Parts List, aero screens are very rare and the author has only seen one example (on a 100S car).

57. Basic "Le Mans" engine modification kit. Double valve springs became standard on all 100 engines from the beginning of volume production. Not shown are the high compression pistons which were also part of the kit.

58. Engine with "Le Mans" conversion. Visual differences over standard engine are twin $1^3/4$ inch carburettors, with 4 stud fixing to enlarged inlet manifold stubs and aluminium cold air box with trunking to air intake behind the radiator grille.

59. The author competing in one of the special tests on the Austin Apprentices Car Club "Donald Healey Trophy" night rally in November 1954.

60. Brussels surgeon Dr. Marek Szpalski in action with his 100M at the eighth European Historic Grand Prix at Zolder in August 1982. (Courtesy Dr. Marek Szpalski).

61

62

61. Within the first year of its general availability on the Home Market, the 100 became quite a popular rally car. This August 1953 registered car, owned and driven by Mr and Mrs Ian Walker, is seen on the Hastings seafront at the end of the MCC/Redex National Rally in November 1954. (Courtesy Ian Walker).

62. How often does one see a dirty Healey today? This is Ian Walker's former car again, this time in action on the fifth RAC Rally in March 1955. Knowledgeable enthusiasts will recognise the location as Pardon Hairpin at Prescott Hill, Gloucestershire. This car has survived and has been well restored by West Country enthusiast Simon Whippel. (Courtesy Ian Walker).

63. The Gordon Wilkins/Marcel Bequart 100 at the 1953 Le Mans 24 hour race. This car covered 2152 miles at an average speed of 87.5mph to take 14th place overall. The other team car averaged 89.6mph for 12th place. (Courtesy Autocar).

64. Geoff Keep's beautifully restored BN1 seen at the 1985 "Classic Prescott" hillclimb, is a regular and effective performer at this meeting. (Courtesy: Stuart Johnson, USA.)

63

64